MAKE MONEY

with

SMALL INCOME
PROPERTIES

MAKE MONEY

with

SMALL INCOME PROPERTIES

GARY W. ELDRED, Ph.D.

WILEY

John Wiley & Sons

Copyright © 2003 by Gary W. Eldred. All rights reserved.

Published by John Wiley & Sons, Inc., Hoboken, New Jersey.
Published simultaneously in Canada.

For general information on our other products and services, please contact our Customer Care Department within the United States at (800) 762-2974, outside the United States at (317) 572-3993 or fax (317) 572-4002.

Wiley also publishes its books in a variety of electronic formats. Some content that appears in print may not be available in electronic books. For more information about Wiley products, visit our Web site at www.wiley.com.

Library of Congress Cataloging-In-Publication Data:

Eldred, Gary W.
   Make money with small income properties / Gary W. Eldred.
     p. cm.
   Includes index.
   ISBN 0-471-43341-1 (pbk.)
   1. Real estate investment—United States.   2. Rental housing—United States.   3. Apartment houses—United States.   4. Real estate management—United States.   I. Title.

HD255.E37524 2003
322.63'243—dc21   2003045097

Printed in the United States of America.
10 9 8 7 6 5 4 3 2 1

CONTENTS

I NTRODUCTION

What You Need to Get Started

You've probably heard it said a hundred times, "It takes money to make money." Not true. To make money with small income properties you only need analytical abilities, an entrepreneurial spirit, and market savvy. When you learn how to recognize good deals, the money will find you. And in this book, like no other, you're going to learn how to find, create, and profit with good deals.

Develop Your Analytical Abilities

Whereas virtually anyone with an IQ above 100 can pretty well estimate the market value of a house by looking at a half dozen similar houses in the same neighborhood that have recently sold, valuing rental properties requires more specialized skills. You will seldom find two income properties that match each other as closely as houses do. With income properties, you must pay attention to details and numbers.

> **Learn to outsmart the competition.**

That's why this book will go into analytical concepts with more precision than most other real estate books. You will learn to truly understand market values, cash flows, income statements, property features, and locations. You will learn to see with critical *and* opportunistic eyes. You will also discover how to judge the strength of the local economy that supports property values, rent levels, and appreciation.

As a reward, after you have become familiar with these concepts and techniques, you will be able to choose those properties that are almost guaranteed to yield strong returns.

Guru Hype versus the Real World

Contrary to the infomercials, buying real estate won't make you money. You will make money when you learn to buy smart, manage effectively, and create value. Many of the real estate hy-pesters and hucksters—those folks who are widely known for their "no cash, no credit, no problem" pitches to the masses—lead the naïve and gullible to believe that if you buy real estate, the money will come. While a few souls may luck out by simply show-ing up in the right place at the right time, only those investors who are protected by a guardian angel should count on serendipity to see them through the fiercely competitive real estate marketplace.

> **Hucksters mislead the naïve.**

All others must count on intelligence (analytical abilities), en-trepreneurial spirit, and market savvy. If you don't carefully con-sider what you're doing, you're likely to get fleeced.

Viewed from a different perspective, this fact spells opportunity. Here's why: When you do develop the appropriate abilities, attitudes, and skills, real estate will offer you virtually unlimited potential.

Develop an Entrepreneurial Spirit

In the popular mind, the term entrepreneur means risk taker. Don't believe it. Through analytic and opportunistic thinking, entrepreneurs actually decrease risk while magnifying their gains. To achieve this result entrepreneurs never cease their quest to find a better way, entrepreneurs develop inquisitive habits of mind: They question. They experiment. They consistently and persistently remain alert to new information, new opportunities.

Uncommon, Yet Essential

This entrepreneurial spirit doesn't come easily to most people. You must work to nurture it. Whenever you look at a property, the entrepreneurial spirit should urge you to blend critical judgment with visionary imagination. Rather than merely critique what's wrong, brainstorm as to remedial possibilities. Rather than accept clichéd advice or so-called standard operating procedures, entrepreneurs ask why or why not.

> **Learn to think like an entrepreneur.**

Now think about it. What is your current entrepreneurial quotient? Do you typically fill your day with nonproductive complaints, gripes, and frustration? Do you tend to quickly reject and pass by new ideas and different ways of seeing or doing? Do you believe that you pretty much know all you need to know? Or do you eagerly try to add to your base of knowledge and experiences?

In his thought-provoking book, *What To Say When You Talk to Your Self* (Pocket Books, 1982), Shad Helmstetter points to many habits of speech that block people from achieving their goals. This nationally prominent psychologist shows how most of us in one way or another erect "walls of negative self-talk" that unconsciously and severely limit what we do and what we're willing to try.

> **Eliminate your self-denying self-talk.**

Pay close attention to your language. Even better, invite comments from others. What patterns of speech, what words and phrases, what limiting beliefs do others notice you using? Worst of all, do you procrastinate? (See Box I.1.)

Someday I should write a list
Of all the deals that I have missed;
Bonanzas that were in my grip—
I watched them through my fingers slip;
The windfalls which I should have
    bought
Were lost because I overthought
I thought of this, I thought of that,
I could have sworn I smelled a rat,
And while I thought things over twice,
Another grabbed them at the price.
It seems I always hesitate,
Then make my mind up much to late.
A very cautious man am I
And that is why I wait to buy.

When tracks rose high on Sixth
    and Third,
The price asked, I felt, was absurd;
Those blockfronts—bleak and black
    with soot—
Were priced at thirty bucks a foot!
I wouldn't even make a bid,
But others did—yes, others did!
When Tucson was cheap desert land,
I could have had a heap of sand;
When Phoenix was the place to buy,
I thought the climate was too dry;
"Invest in Dallas—that's the spot!"
My sixth sense warned me I should not.
A very prudent man am I
And that is why I wait to buy.

How Nassau and how Suffolk grew!
North Jersey! Staten Island, too!
When others culled these
    sprawling farms
And welcomed deals with open arms . . .
A corner here, ten acres there,
Compounding values year by year,
I chose to think and as I thought,
They bought the deals I should have
    bought.
The golden chances I had then
Are lost and will not come again.
Today I cannot be enticed
For everything's so overpriced.
The deals of yesteryear are dead;
The market's soft—and so's my head.

Last night I had a fearful dream,
I know I wakened with a scream:
Some Indians approached my bed—
For trinkets on the barrelhead
(In dollar bills worth twenty-four
And nothing less and nothing more)
They'd sell Manhattan Isle to me.
The most I'd go was twenty-three.
The redmen scowled: "Not on a bet!"
And sold to Peter Minuit.

At times a teardrop drowns my eye
For deals I had, but did not buy;
And now life's saddest words I pen—
"IF ONLY I'D INVESTED THEN!"

—Anonymous

The moral: Don't wait to buy real esate. Buy real estate and wait.

Box I.1   Investor's Regret.

Entrepreneurs Create Value for Themselves and Their Customers (a.k.a. Tenants)

Throughout this book, I will try to fire up your imagination. I will offer suggestions that you can use to enhance your investment possibilities. And, as is explained later, I will give you a system of strategic thinking that can help you formulate and evaluate profitable plans of action.

But when all is said and done, your profitable property operations and improvements will grow from your enthusiasm and desire to provide your targeted tenants (customers) with an outstanding value proposition—a value proposition that these tenants will eagerly prefer over those offered by all other competing properties and property owners.

Good strategy begins with wanting to do good. It's as much emotional (passion) as it is intellectual. To succeed where others fail, first truly feel the drive to persistently do better.

Market Savvy: Systematic Strategic Thinking

Try this experiment: Talk with run-of-the-mill property managers, owners, and investors. Ask them how they come up with the market strategy that will maximize their cash flows as well as their long-term property values. Their answers, at best, will display some random combination of experience, seat-of-the-pants judgment, and creative insight. Sure, at most times and in most markets, investors who have approached their so-called strategy in this offhand way do eventually succeed. Steady rent increases, property appreciation, and a paid-off mortgage do produce long-term returns.

But these investors don't make nearly as much money as they could. They suffer more headaches and hassles than necessary. And for many, when storms hit, their boat capsizes. How do I know? Because for more than 20 years, I've worked as a market and financial consultant to homebuilders, developers, investors, and realty firms. In addition, I've bought, renovated, managed, and sold dozens of rental properties for my own account.

> **Do well by doing good.**

In all of this experience, I've never seen a situation where profits could not be enhanced through a better, more systematic approach to strategy and execution. The evidence I've accumulated clearly proves that you will dramatically increase your returns and alleviate your risks when you systematically organize your thinking, data gathering, and operating plans. After you've intelligently adopted this approach, you will see how to blend market analysis with systematic, goal-oriented thinking to outperform competing owners and investors whether you're facing good times or bad.

If all of this market analysis and strategic thinking sounds like work, you're right—up to a point. But after you set up your system and develop a plan to keep it current, your day-to-day efforts will diminish and your rewards will multiply. As with most other professional learning, throughout your career of real estate investing, a relatively small amount of effort up front will pay big dividends over time. Even better, you will discover that you can easily find much of the market, economic, and property data that you will need. Government agencies, Realtors, property management firms, utility companies, and other sources routinely collect and publish valuable information about real estate and local economic trends.

And in the end, it is you who will decide how much data to include in your strategy making. On some of my consulting assignments, I've put in as much as three months full-time. But even if you invest just three days to gain market savvy, the returns from your investments will show a marked improvement. You will achieve this result because your entrepreneurial spirit, market savvy, and strategic thinking will power your performance—over your competitors who fly by the seat of their pants.

> **Earn superior returns through strategic marketing.**

Stephen Covey emphasizes, "Begin with the end in mind and you will multiply the effectiveness of any given degree of effort." Amen! To maximize your profits in real estate, develop a strategic plan for every property you own—before you buy it.

CHAPTER 1

Profit with Income Properties

In this chapter, you will learn why owning small income properties will make you wealthy. In this context, I use the term *small income properties* to mean multifamily apartment buildings that range in size from duplexes up to, say, 24 units.

You can acquire properties that fall within this category for as little as $15,000 per unit (or even less). But more commonly, you will probably pay a price of $25,000 to $50,000 per unit. In higher-priced cities and neighborhoods, such properties may sell in the range of $50,000 to $100,000 per unit. Even within the same city, you will find that price-per-unit figures will vary by neighborhood, property condition, and type of tenant. In every location, though, when compared to houses, multi-unit properties tend to offer investors lower prices, high cash flows, and numerous other advantages. You can get a feel for the types of properties I'm talking about from Figure 1.1.

Advantages of Multi-Unit Properties

Most small real estate investors begin their entry into the field with single-family houses. This step seems easiest and most familiar

Property Description	Sq. Ft.	Price	Net Income	Cap Rate
Gold Canyon, AZ *Eight-unit* two-story building. All two bedrooms one bath. ($49,375 p.u.)	4,000	$395,000	$35,550	.09
San Pablo, CA *Four-plex* with rec. room and pool room and television room. Area has bar-bq and hot tub. Covered parking. Units are 100% occupied. ($243,750 p.u.)	5,632	$975,000	$70,200	.072
Spokane, WA *Unique property* on Spokane's lower South Hill. *Six 5-unit* buildings adjacent and contiguous. Ample parking in the rear of the property. ($29,833 p.u.)	18,000	$895,000	$79,655	.089
Fort Wayne, IN Newly remodeled 5 one-bedroom apartments. *All new mechanicals, all new appliances, new windows and carpet.* ($30,000 p.u.)	3,800	$150,000	$16,200	.108
Akron, OH *(2) two*-bedroom apartments, *(1) one*-bedroom, *(1) efficiency* plus 3-car garage with circular driveway. Rents 450×2; $275; $255. ($32,250 p.u.)	2,988	$129,000	$11,115	.085
Evanston, IL This vintage building consists of *10 very large apartments.* ($160,000 p.u.)	18,350	$1,600,000	$96,000	.06
Miami, FL *Triplex.* Section 8 qualified. Good condition. ($49,967 p.u.)	2,400	$149,900	$18,744	.125

Figure 1.1   A Sampling of Pricing and Location for Small Residential Income Properties.

Property Description	Sq. Ft.	Price	Net Income	Cap Rate
Cincinnati, OH Brick construction, built in 1921 & renovated in mid 1980s. Very large units. *21 total units,* 15 two-bdrms (1,000 SF to 1,384 SF) and 6 . . . ($23,095 p.u.)	38,788	$485,000	$58,200	.12
Trenton, NJ *One retail storefront and five apartments.* Fully leased corner property. ($41,500 p.u.)	4,330	$249,000	$31,623	.127
Holyoke, MA *22 2-BR apartments.* Lead paint compliant! Brick four-story. 100% occupied. ($27,000 p.u.)	27,914	$594,000	$67,716	.114

For a broader sampling of properties, prices, and cap rates, visit loopnet.com.

Figure 1.1 *(Continued)*

because most of these people have already bought their own personal residence. Buying a single-family house to rent out basically repeats this same purchase process.

However, even though I have owned many rental houses, I actually began my investing with a five-unit property, followed that purchase with a seven-unit property, and next added a four-unit to my portfolio. Novice investors need not fear "getting in over their heads" with apartment properties. In fact, I recently told a medical doctor in Atlanta who had asked me for advice that he should look for a 4- to 12-unit property rather than the single-family rentals that he was currently exploring. My reasons for this advice include the following:

- ◆ Low cost of acquisition
- ◆ Higher cash flows
- ◆ Less search time

◆ Greater ease of management
◆ Increased tax-free, trade-up potential
◆ More potential for owner financing
◆ Enhanced possibilities for creating value

Let's look at each of these advantages a little more closely.

Lower Cost of Acquisition

The median price of a single-family house in the United States has now climbed above $160,000. In higher-priced areas such as San Diego, Boston, New York, and Washington, D.C., the median price approaches $300,000. Unless you want to invest in less desirable neighborhoods—and even there, house prices can seem absurd, such as in East Palo Alto, California, or Chicago Southside—investing in single-family housing is becoming cost prohibitive for many investors of average means.

Hopeful homebuyers, too, have noticed the cost advantages of small income properties. As a result, owner-occupied duplexes, triplexes, and quads are again attracting renewed interest.

> **Small income properties appeal to homebuyers and investors.**

Individuals or families who couldn't begin to afford the monthly payments on a $350,000 house now find that they can afford a $500,000 or $600,000 quad because the rent collections will go a long way toward paying their principal, interest, property taxes, and property insurance (PITI).

When I talk with homebuyers priced out of their desired neighborhoods, I tell them to look for a small income property. Buy it. Use rent collections to help meet monthly expenses. Create value through improvements and then sell or trade-up in a few years. This same advice holds true for investors.

Given their lower per-unit prices (relative to single-family houses), small income properties can give you a more affordable entry into real estate. In addition, you will typically achieve higher cash flows with multi-unit properties.

Higher Cash Flows

For most of the past 30 years, many renters were shut out of home ownership because they could not qualify for a mortgage. They either lacked acceptable credit or they had failed to save enough money to cover the down payment and closing costs. This situation worked to the advantage of investors who owned single-family houses. Tenants paid relatively high rents because they had no other choice. Even though "owning was cheaper than renting," tough mortgage standards kept people in rentals. Single-family investors enjoyed high positive cash flows.

The New World of Home Buying The days of positive cash flows for single-family investors have disappeared in many cities. During the past five years, low interest rates, easy-qualify mortgages, and little or nothing down first-time buyer home loans have converted millions of previously discouraged renters into homeowners. This mass conversion of renters into homeowners has hurt would-be investors in single-family houses in two ways: It has pushed home prices up to record highs, thus making purchases less affordable for investors; it has also kept rents from rising. New homebuilders all over the country now advertise with the question: "Why rent when you can own?"

> **Single-family rentals often yield negative cash flows.**

With such fierce (and unprecedented) competition from homebuilders, rent levels for single-family houses have fallen behind the increases in housing prices. Lower rents relative to prices means that most *new* investors must either come up with a 25 to 40 percent down payment or incur negative cash flows.

When I first began to invest, my single-family houses would generate a positive cash flow—even with 100 percent financing.

In those days you could buy houses at a price of 100 times the monthly rent. In other words, you could buy a house for $50,000 and then rent it for $500 per month. Although houses in some areas still yield comparable amounts of cash flow, you will find that, in the more expensive cities, the monthly gross rent multiplier for houses has jumped to 150, 200, or higher.

A house that now rents for $1,000 a month might sell for $150,000, $200,000, or more. To bring in gross rents of $1,500 a month in most major cities, you would need to buy a house priced in the range of $250,000 to $300,000. Although long-time investors in single-family houses are now reaping a bonanza in equity gains due to price appreciation, new investors in rental houses face the worst cash flow situation in memory.

I know because I routinely talk with would-be investors throughout the country. Never before have I encountered so much discouragement, especially from younger investors who want to buy houses to build their wealth. To these investors I say buy "fixers" (see my book, *Make Money with Fixer-Uppers and Renovations*) or, as emphasized in this book, buy small income properties.

> **Priced out of single family? Buy a fixer.**

Apartments Provide Lower GRMs and Thus Higher Cash Flows   Even though single-family houses now often command gross rent multipliers (GRMs) of 150, 200, or higher, you can still find multi-unit properties in most cities that sell for prices of 80 to 135 times gross potential monthly rent collections. As a result, smaller apartment properties (especially 5 to 24 units or larger) can yield a positive cash flow with just 10 to 20 percent down. In fact, as I show later, you can still buy income properties and achieve a 10 to 20 percent cash-on-cash return.

This discrepancy in cash flows persists (at least for the time being) because investors value income properties primarily according to how much cash flow they produce. If a deal

> **Income properties typically yield more rent per dollar invested.**

can't be structured to yield a positive cash flow, most property investors will walk away and look for another property.

In contrast, homebuyers value single-family houses according to their personal tastes and their monthly earnings from their jobs. If homebuyers want the house and they can afford the monthly payments, they will pay whatever price the market will bear; therefore, when buying single-family houses, investors must outbid homebuyers who do not think chiefly in terms of annual cash-on-cash investment returns. When investors ignore cash flow and invest primarily for appreciation, they're no longer *investing*—they're basically speculating on higher prices.

Expect Cash Flows to Fall in the Future   Today, most small income properties can still generate positive cash flows. Will this situation persist? I don't think so—at least not with low down payments.

As boomers continue to fret over the source and adequacy of their retirement incomes, increasing numbers will recognize the advantages of income properties. As more investors search out this type of property, they will bid up prices. Although over time rent levels will continue to inflate, property prices will inflate even faster. Relative to property prices, cash flows (rent collections) will not keep pace. We can already see this trend in cities such as New York and San Francisco. In these and other high-priced locations, speculators in appreciation potential have virtually pushed cash flow investors out of the market.

I recently saw a six-unit property in San Francisco sell for $1.2 million. Rent collections for this property totaled just $7,200 a month. On a monthly basis, this price-rent relationship (the gross rent multiplier) came in at 166. With 20 percent down, the rents would barely cover the mortgage payments (debt service).

That means that these investors must either come up with a much higher down payment or go out-of-pocket each year to pay for property taxes, insurance, maintenance, and repairs. An all-cash purchase of this property would have netted these investors an annual yield of just 4.7 percent (not counting appreciation, which, of course, is where they really planned to make their money).

Fortunately for beginning investors, most cities still offer reasonable cash flows *and* strong potential for appreciation. But don't wait too long. Given that bond interest rates offer very low returns and stocks are clouded with uncertainty, income properties now stand clearly superior to these other popular investments. Yet, with too much money chasing too few good investments, you need to act now. Absent some type of general economic collapse, five years from now, the selling prices of small income properties will have climbed significantly higher, and positive cash flows (under historically normal terms of financing) will be found in fewer and fewer locations.

> **Too much money chasing too few good investments.**

What Yields Are Reasonable?   Throughout the decade of the 1990s, many stock market investors easily earned yields of 12 to 20 percent a year. By the turn of the century, various surveys revealed that most investors had come to believe that they could expect such high yields to continue year after year for as far as the eye could see.

As most people now realize, these grandiose expectations bore no relationship to reality. Because the U.S. economy grows (on average) just 3 to 5 percent a year, it is mathematically impossible for the stock market to grow continuously at a rate three to six times as fast. As we look to the future with clearer vision, virtually all stock hypesters have toned down their rhetoric. Even that great bull Jeremy (*Stocks for the Long Run,* McGraw-Hill, 3rd ed., 2002) Siegel now tells stock investors to prepare for stock market returns of no better than 7 percent a year for at least a decade—and that 7 percent is before deductions for brokerage fees, mutual fund expenses, and income taxes!

Implications for Real Estate   With dividend yields (positive cash flows) on stocks of less than 2 percent a year and total returns of 7 percent (if and when the stock market again moves steadily upwards), investors are longing for higher yields. Yet at present, only real estate (and especially income properties) can offer investors those double-digit returns that for one brief and exceptional moment in history were previously experienced by stocks.

Surprisingly, relatively few investors understand this opportunity. Many still cling to the false hope that stocks will rebound and replay their glory days. Others are pushing money into risky hedge funds or merely sitting on the sidelines with their money market funds primed to pour into the next big thing.

However, this mass ignorance won't persist very far into the future. I know from the sales figures of my own books and talks with readers who call me that increasing numbers of investors are seriously considering real estate. My conversations with real estate agents around the country also reveal heightened interest in real estate by investors. As noted earlier, most of this newly generated interest centers on single-family housing—until, that is, these would-be investors discover the reality of negative cash flows.

> **Property prices will go up as investors search for yield.**

To counter this problem, many new real estate investors have begun to search for foreclosures, distressed owners, and fixer-uppers. Several best-selling books have led people to believe that they can routinely buy real estate "wholesale" at discounts off "retail" of 30 to 40 percent. Naturally, increased competition for these types of properties makes good deals tougher to find. So what other options can beginning investors pursue? Small income properties and condominiums, which I explain in my book, *Make Money with Condominiums and Townhouses*. But as the merits of these properties as investments become more widely known, opportunities here will also become relatively less rewarding for new investors.

Twenty years ago, fewer than 10 million Americans were seriously saving and investing for retirement, their kids' college education, and other longer-term financial goals. Today, that number has grown to 50 million or more.

It doesn't take an Einstein to figure out that because the middle class has joined the moneyed class in pursuit of solid investments, cash yields will continue to fall. It defies reason to believe that 50 million Americans can all find safe investments that yield cash-on-cash returns of 15, 12, or even 10 percent a year.

> **All investment cash-on-cash yields will continue to fall.**

This is why I urge you to get started now. Even though the cash flow returns today don't look as good as they did 5 or 10 years ago, they look far better today than they will look 5 or 10 years into the future. The total number of investors searching for high yields has grown far faster than the capacity of the economy to generate high investment returns. Mathematically, the majority of these investors must end up disappointed.

Less Search Time

In contrast to single-family houses, you can build wealth in multi-unit properties with far less search time. Even in high-cost areas, a $5,000,000 or $10,000,000 portfolio of houses would (or at least should) include at least 20 or 30 separate properties. In lower-priced areas, a portfolio of this amount might include as many as 50 or 100 separate properties. Obviously, to buy that many houses would require at least several thousand hours of looking at homes, evaluating neighborhoods, negotiating purchase contracts, and applying for loans.

> **Build unlimited wealth with income properties, yet invest less time and effort.**

With smaller income properties, though, you can work your way up to a $5,000,000 or $10,000,000 dollar portfolio with as few as 3 to 10 acquisitions. Even if each multi-unit deal takes two or three times as long to complete as a single-family purchase, you've still saved a considerable amount of search time. Of course, as you move up to a 20, 30, or 50 million dollar portfolio of properties (should you plan to grow that wealthy), such a large collection of single-family houses would become virtually impossible to acquire and manage. For real estate investors who want a life apart from making money, multi-unit properties give far more investment return for each hour invested in property acquisitions and negotiations.

Greater Ease of Management

When you own 15 or 20 houses, you've got 15 or 20 furnaces, roofs, air conditioners, electrical systems, and yards to oversee. If you own two or three multi-unit buildings instead, you cut down the components that at some point will need attention. Although maintaining a multi-family property will cost more per building, it will cost you less per unit both in terms of dollars and time.

In addition, as you move up to 12- to 24-unit buildings or larger, you can afford to employ an on-site manager who will attend to any day-to-day concerns that arise. You can compensate your on-site manager(s) with a nominal amount of rent reduction. Ideally, your on-site people should perform some maintenance and repairs, address most tenant problems or concerns, and prepare and lease vacancies as they occur. Overall, you will find that you can operate 50 units of a multi-family property as easily as you might manage 5 or 10 single-family rental houses. With on-site help and efficient procedures, managing multi-unit properties on a continuous basis need not require much of your personal time or effort.

Increased Tax-Free Trade-Up Potential

To build wealth, you must avoid paying taxes to the maximum extent that the law allows. For owners of multi-unit properties, the Internal Revenue Code offers a generous advantage. As you move up to larger properties, you can pyramid your wealth-building tax-free through a Section 1031 tax-deferred exchange.

If you *sell* a property, you must pay a tax on your gain; therefore, the amount you can reinvest in a larger property is reduced by the amount of taxes owed. With a Section 1031 exchange, however, you preserve your gain and your total accumulated equity counts toward your down payment on the larger property.

> **Never pay tax on capital gains.**

Exchanges Don't Necessarily Involve Two-Way Trades   Owing to lack of knowledge, most real estate investors who have some awareness of tax-free exchanges believe that to use this tax benefit, they must find a seller who will accept one or more of their currently owned properties in trade. Although this possibility represents one way to complete a tax-free exchange, it does not represent the most commonly used exchange technique. Most exchanges actually involve at least three investors.

The Three-Party Exchange   Three-party exchanges outnumber two-party "trade-in" exchanges because it's usually difficult to find an owner of a property you want who will accept the property you plan to trade up. True, it's sometimes possible to persuade an unwilling seller to accept your property in trade. But to do so may cause you to spend too much negotiating capital that you could otherwise devote to issues such as a lower price or owner-will-carry (OWC) financing.

> **Exchanges can involve several property owners who simultaneously buy and sell.**

Instead, most serious real estate investors arrange a three-party exchange through the following steps: Locate a buyer for the property you want to trade; locate a property you want to buy; and set up an escrow whereby you deed your property to your buyer, the buyer pays cash to your seller, and your seller conveys the property to you. In effect, no property has really been "exchanged" for another property. Because of this anomaly, John Reed (a leading expert on exchanges) suggests renaming this technique the "interdependent sale and reinvestment" strategy. As you might guess, Reed's suggested nomenclature has not caught on.

Exchanges Are Complex but Easy   Anything that involves federal tax laws will be entangled in a spider web of rules and regulations, and Section 1031 exchanges prove no exception. However, even though exchange rules are complex, exchange transactions are relatively easy to administer when you work with a professional who is experienced in successfully setting up and carrying out tax-free exchanges.

John Reed says the total extra costs (including attorney fees and escrow charges) of conducting an exchange should not exceed $2,000. Professional Publishing Company (now taken over by Dearborn Financial in Chicago) even publishes standard forms that may be used to complete the required paperwork according to law. Even if you rely on standards forms, use a tax or realty exchange professional. Be aware that the great majority of certified public accountants (CPAs) and real estate attorneys know little about Section 1031 exchanges. Unless you accountant or lawyer has mastered this area of the law, find someone else who has this expertise. If you live in at least a midsize city, there's probably an exchange club whose members include investors and commercial realty brokers who can recommend competent and experienced exchange professionals.

> **Upward exchanges do not result in taxable gains.**

Are Tax-Free Exchanges Really Tax Free?
Some people quibble with the term "tax-free exchange." They say that an exchange doesn't eliminate taxes but only defers payment to a later date. This view is wrong on five counts:

1.   The exchange itself is tax free if you follow the rules.
2.   Whether you must pay taxes at a later date depends on how you divest yourself of the property. If you hold it until death, the property passes into your estate free of any capital gains taxes.

3. As another alternative, you could arrange a sale in a later year in which you have tax losses that you can use to offset the amount of your capital gain.

4. You can withdraw your equity through a tax-free cash-out refinance.

5. If Americans are sensible enough to elect legislators who understand the importance of productive investment, we may see the income tax—or at least the capital gains tax–abolished.

The most important point is that exchanges eliminate capital gains in the year you dispose of an income property by trading up. Whether you pay in future years will depend on how savvy you are in developing your tax-avoidance strategies and on the tax law that exists in some future year. By exchanging, you eliminate a definite tax liability in the year of disposition and accept an uncertain and contingent future tax liability. That's a tax trade-off you should always try to make.

Single-Family Houses   Technically, you can also use a Section 1031 tax-deferred exchange to avoid taxes when you acquire more expensive houses or even to trade up from a single-family house to a multi-unit property. As a practical matter, though, this technique is pursued far more with multi-unit properties than with single-family houses. Experienced multi-unit investors readily enter into such agreements and are well acquainted with its advantages. Owners of single-family residences are much less likely to have experience in this area and will tend to reject the unknown and unfamiliar.

> **You can also trade-up single-family rental houses and condos tax-free.**

Nevertheless, if you do own or plan to own rental houses, don't overlook the Section 1031 possibility. As noted, if you want to move up from one or more single-family residences to multi-unit buildings, try to structure the transaction to avoid those nasty, equity-reducing taxes on capital gains.

More Potential for Owner Financing

In the world of real estate, OWC financing nearly always beats bank financing. Owners generally structure their deals with less red tape, easier qualifying, more flexible (creative) terms, and lower closing costs. Also, sellers will frequently accept lower down payments. Although some sellers of single-family houses will finance their buyers, this practice stands far more common in the field of multi-unit properties. In fact, nearly all of my multi-unit acquisitions have involved at least some seller financing.

> **Owners often offer seller-assisted financing to investors.**

Nevertheless, as the real estate investor and columnist Robert Bruss has pointed out, many owners don't volunteer OWC financing. To get it, you must make OWC part of your purchase offer and then explain why it makes sense from the seller's point of view. Overall, OWC can often help you close multi-unit deals with financing terms that would never pass muster with a bank underwriter.

Enhanced Possibilities for Creating Value

Although you can certainly create value through improvements with single-family residences, your possibilities for doing so increase substantially with multi-unit properties. With single-family houses, you're bidding against homebuyers. Because most homebuyers don't factor a profit margin into their purchase offers, they tend to pay too much for properties in need of work or other types of improvements.

In contrast, professionals dominate the multi-unit market. These investors will run the numbers very closely. Without a strong profit potential, they will turn down the deal. As a result, bidding wars and overpaying result less frequently. To attract a buyer, sellers of multi-unit properties must be willing to cut their price or give other incentives to assure smart buyers they can earn a profit.

Types of Improvements   In terms of actual improvements, multi-unit properties also give you greater leeway. With single-family houses, tight zoning laws, the character of the neighborhood, and the prices of nearby houses all conspire to limit your upside potential. With multi-unit properties, value relates directly to the amount of net income the property produces. Anything you can do to boost net income will boost the value of the property. Because multi-unit buildings are typically regulated by less restrictive zoning laws, you typically enjoy a wider array of profit-generating possibilities.

> Income properties multiply your opportunities to create value.

Moreover, effective management counts far more toward creating value for multi-unit properties vis-à-vis a single-family house. A house is worth what a house is worth. Management per se counts little. The great majority of homebuyers plan to live in the house, not rent it out. With multi-unit buildings, however, management exerts control over operating costs, tenant satisfaction, tenant turnover, rent collections, and overall market strategy. Together, these and many other variables determine the cash flow that the income property will produce and, correspondingly, its value.

Even better, at least in terms of your opportunities, most owners of small income properties poorly manage their buildings. To verify this fact for yourself, look at some properties. Talk with tenants. You'll nearly always find great room for improvement. We'll go over many value-creating techniques in later chapters, but for now, realize that many (if not most) small income properties offer great potential for turnaround and higher net incomes.

Economies of Scale   As with acquisition and management, income properties also offer economies of scale when it comes to making improvements. To improve, say, 12 houses, you will need to work with 12 different buildings in 12 different locations. Each property will require its own unique market research, design, repairs, and renovations. In contrast, you can improve one 12-unit (or two 6-unit) properties with much less time and effort (per rental unit).

Your renovation costs will also reflect economies of scale. One large roof costs far less than 12 individual roofs. To the extent that each of a building's individual units are similar, you can apply just one redesign to all of the units. When you focus on one (two, or even three) larger properties instead of a dozen or more smaller properties, you again achieve more return for each hour you invest.

Summing Up

In looking to the years ahead, I'm convinced that real estate investors who at one time would have thought only about single-family houses will be switching their interest to small, multi-unit properties. These investments provide significant economies of scale, cost less per unit, yield higher annual cash flows, and present greater opportunities for creating value and management turnaround. At present, when compared to stocks, bonds, annuities, or any other income-oriented assets, small income properties seem destined to produce superior performance.

> **Small income properties yield superior performance.**

Put into practice the strategic principles and techniques laid out in the following chapters and you will achieve both a high net worth and a solid, inflation-protected income for life. Best of all, your tenants will love you.

CHAPTER 2

Craft Your Entrepreneurial Strategy

Ever since William Nickerson wrote his now classic *How I Turned $1,000 into a Million in my Spare Time* (Pocket Books, 1959), best-selling real estate authors have been revealing "the secrets of my success." To name just a few who have (more or less) followed this approach: Suzanne Thomas, Robert Allen, Leigh Robinson, Robert Irwin, Kevin Meyers, Roger Neal, David Schumacher, and yes, even yours truly, Gary Eldred. In fact, you may already have read books written by one or more of these author-investors.

But here's the catch: If you simply adopt an investment approach that was developed by someone else in another place and time, you may end up losing your bank account. And without a doubt, you will certainly miss the best opportunities that present themselves to you (albeit, often unannounced). Why? Because real estate markets experience continuous change.

Look at such important variables as interest rates; vacancy rates; property prices; rent levels; employment; population demographics, consumer tastes, preferences attitudes, and lifestyles; the cost and supply of new construction; and government zoning rules, regulations, and restrictions. These variables and dozens of others not only shift across time but also across states, cities, and metropolitan areas.

Just recently, an investor asked me if HUD's Section Eight rental program was worth pursuing. I answered, "It all depends." In Orange County, Florida, I'm told that most rental property owners won't go near the program. In contrast, in the nearby county of Seminole, some investors say they love it. Section Eight provides a clear path to profits.

It All Depends

To their detriment, more than a few naïve (gullible?) investor wannabes would like to believe that someone else can tell them

> **No one can tell you the easy way to real estate riches.**

exactly what they need to do to make a fortune in real estate. But life's not that easy. Yes, you can learn from the experiences of others; you can certainly get ideas that you may want to try. Serious real estate investors should read everything they can find that might lead to improved performance.

Nevertheless, before you jump to follow a popular real estate guru, remember three of the most important words in real estate (and life)—It all depends!

A Strategy of Your Own

In this book, I won't mislead you with "five magic paths" or "seven easy steps" to real estate riches. I won't give you a list of detailed dos and don'ts. And I won't pretend that you can profitably buy, improve, and manage income properties without some investment of effort, time, intelligence, and at least a workable amount of seed capital.[1]

---

1. This money does not necessarily have to come from your pocket. Partners or relatives frequently provide seed capital and credit for both beginning and experienced real estate investors.

However, I do promise to share the knowledge and techniques necessary for you to develop a profitable, wealth-building strategy of your own. In the real world, you will conquer the challenges and vicissitudes of income property investing only when you know how to discover current market facts and adapt as problems arise and opportunities unfold. In other words, from this book—as with no other—you will learn to think strategically.

PVP: The One Constant Rule

To think strategically, you adopt one central marketing rule: I call this unifying rule (or principle), the preferred value proposition (PVP). When tenants shop for a place to live, they compare features, amenities, location, rent levels, lease terms, and perhaps dozens of other details that will add to (or detract from) their enjoyment of a property. They compare, contrast, weigh, and consider. In the end, which property do they eventually choose? The cheapest? Not necessarily. The best? Probably not. The biggest? Maybe, but you can't count on it.

> **Offer your target market superior value.**

In the final analysis, you can only say that tenants will choose the property that offers the total value proposition that they prefer over all of the other properties that they have considered.

"Okay," you might say, "what's new here, Eldred? You're only stating the obvious." To that I respond both yes and no. Yes because in one sense, everyone knows that (absent coercion) people will choose their best deal. But when it comes to the actual practices of property owners, manager, and renovators, I answer an emphatic NO!

During the past 20 years, I have looked at more than 5,000 (for rent, for sale) properties throughout the United States, Canada, Mexico, and Australia. Without a doubt, at least 90 percent of these properties would have benefited from better marketing.

And by "better marketing" I don't simply mean better advertising or better salesmanship. Instead, I mean the total strategic effort.

I mean that the property's owner, manager, or sales agent had not adequately or systematically addressed the question of PVP. Namely, "How might we enhance our value proposition in ways that would better satisfy (amaze) our customers (tenants, buyers) and at the same time pull more dollars through to our bottom line?"

Remember, before you can improve in any area of life, you must want to improve. You must be willing to make the required effort. You must believe that the effort will pay off. You must develop an entrepreneurial attitude. Accordingly, the latter chapters of this book provide the profit-enhancing pointers and insights that you can integrate into your overall market and investment strategy and thus create a PVP for your tenants-to-be. But first, let's go through a quick summary of the strategic framework.

The Dust Strategic Framework: A Quick Overview

Look at Figure 2.1.[2] From this diagram you can quickly grasp the strategic reasoning process that I advocate. Essentially, it combines these five elements:

1. Know thyself.
2. Set up your analysis.
3. Systematically collect pertinent data.
4. Develop your market strategy.
5. Plan your work. Execute your plan.

Originally, I developed a variant of the demand, utility, scarcity, and transfer (DUST) strategic framework to help in my consulting with major clients such as Wells Fargo, Century 21 International, Georgia Pacific, and Pebble Creek Development, but eventually I realized that individual real estate investors could use a similar

---

2. As you will notice, the acronym DUST refers to the four key areas that savvy investors must investigate: (1) *Demand*, (2) *Utility*, (3) *Supply*, and (4) *Transfer* process.

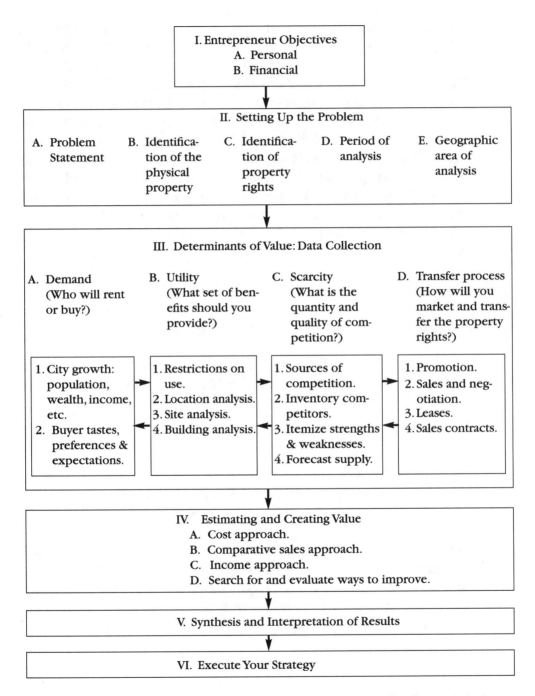

Figure 2.1   DUST Strategic Framework (© Gary W. Eldred, reprinted with permission).

thought process to greatly improve their own market and investment strategies. So I wrote a college text book aimed specifically at
business school students who were taking a course in real estate
market and investment analysis.[3]

Subsequently, after writing this book *(Real Estate: Analysis
and Strategy),* I was invited to teach this system in the graduate
business programs at Stanford University, the University of Virginia,
and several other top-ranked colleges. I've also taught the system in
various investment seminars and programs that have been offered to
investors, property development companies, and market consultants.

> **Planned strategy
> beats generic.**

Overall, considerable positive feedback confirms that this strategic system really works to
help investors discover and exploit their best
market opportunities. In later examples, I will
show how I and others have used this type of
strategic reasoning to boost rents and enhance
the values of small income properties.

As noted previously, you will decide for yourself how much analytical detail is necessary to serve your purposes, yet you should
know that investor results do prove that even casual application of
this strategic framework will multiply your returns. In other words,
you can simply buy properties and rent them out. This generic approach will give you generic returns. Or you can get to know yourself as well as your local markets, properties, tenants, and economic
conditions. You then develop a specific strategy that's tailored to
your resources, goals, and the most promising market opportunities. By putting this approach into action, you will not only magnify
your profits—you will also minimize your risks.

Entrepreneur Objectives: Know Thyself

Nearly everyone wants to make money. Especially now, as stock
market dreams (and stock portfolios) dissipate, many investors

---

3. For much greater detail than permitted here, see *Real Estate: Analysis and Strategy* (Harper &
Row, 1987).

have made a mad rush into real estate. But before you merely run with the herd, take measure of your personal and financial resources, your talents, and your objectives. You can then choose an investment program and market strategy that will best serve your purposes and your desired style of life.

Talents, Inclinations, and Resources

When I first began buying and renovating properties, I not only lacked a clear plan, I also failed to inventory my talents and inclinations. Only after trial and error did I manage to stick with real estate and eventually developed an investment program that worked for me both personally and financially. Unfortunately, too many would-be real estate investors choose the wrong program, or the wrong way to execute, and then give up before they've given the field a fair chance.

Before you commit to a course of action, realistically review how well your investing will align with your personal abilities, resources, likes, and dislikes. For starters, ask yourself the following questions:

1. *Time and money.* How many hours per week or per month are you willing to invest? Realistically, what does your financial profile look like (credit, cash, earnings, borrowing power)?
2. *Trade skills.* What types of handyman talents do you possess? Do you enjoy this type of work?
3. *Creativity and design.* Do you enjoy searching out new ideas? Are you willing to learn and adapt the ideas of other? Would you like looking at properties, attending trade shows, and browsing through magazines and journals on property management, creative improvements, and related topics?
4. *Partners.* Do you prefer to play as a one-man band, or would you like to join with others to share equity financing, work, responsibilities, and decision making?

5. ***Tenants.*** What types of people would you like to attract as tenants?

6. ***Real estate agents.*** Do you want to search and sell on your own, or will you enlist the help of real estate agents?

7. ***Numbers.*** Can you learn to work with income statements, cash flows, rate of return calculations, cost estimates, budgets, and tight rehab and renovation schedules?

8. ***Personal achievement.*** What types of real estate would give you the greatest sense of personal achievement and pride of accomplishment and ownership?

No matter how you answer each of these questions, you can develop a strategy that more or less fits your desired profile, but the key to success is to anticipate and prepare, to harbor and hold expectations that match reality. Too many owners of small income properties try to "do it all." They burn out long before they realize their potential. Others buy with "little or nothing down" and then find they lack the cash or credit necessary to get through stormy weather. On the positive side, these mismatches of time, talent, and money often produce distressed sellers who sell at bargain prices—"just to get rid of this headache."

> **Their loss becomes your gain.**

Assess Your Finances

The nothing-down real estate promoters have pulled too many starry-eyed investor wannabes further down the path to financial ruin with their mantra of "no cash, no credit, no problem." Although it's certainly true that you can buy real estate without cash or credit, that fact begs the question: If that's your situation, why don't you have any cash or credit?

To succeed in real estate (as with all other types of investing), you need to exercise financial discipline and responsibility. "No cash, no credit" is certainly a problem if your impecunious position results from excessive spending and borrowing.

Because I've written extensively on this topic elsewhere, I won't repeat myself here. But please, never believe for a moment that investing in real estate will put you on the road to financial freedom absent a diligent capacity to save and spend wisely.[4]

Financial Position   To manage your finances as a borderline miser, you should assess your credit capacity, available cash, and regular monthly cash flow. How much money will you be able to allocate to real estate acquisitions and fix-up work while still maintaining a reserve to cover contingencies and emergencies? Because you run some chance of committing beginner's mistakes, don't push your limits. Use your first properties to gain experience and fine-tune your strategy. To really see where you currently stand financially, answer these questions.

What is your credit score?   In their efforts to determine whether you're a good credit risk, most mortgage lenders will run your credit score. Although numerous credit-scoring systems now exist, the most widely used score is calculated by the Fair, Isaacs Company (FICO). To learn your FICO score, go to www.myfico.com. For $12.95, Fair Isaacs will tell you your score and suggest ways you can improve it. It will also let you know how your score compares to everyone else and, based on your actual credit profile, this Web site will give you some idea about the interest rate that lenders would charge you. (The higher your credit score, the lower your interest rate and vice versa.)

> **Check your credit score.**

What is your net worth?   Essentially, your net worth consists of the total value of what you own less the total amount you owe to others.

---

4. For a good book that describes the personal discipline necessary to become wealthy, see *The Millionaire Next Door* (Longstreet, 1997).

(If you've previously completed a mortgage application, you're probably familiar with this form, which is called a *personal balance sheet.*)

How liquid are you?   Mortgage lenders won't just focus on your total assets and net worth; they will also want to evaluate your cash position. Generally, the more cash you have on hand, the better you can meet adverse times and unanticipated setbacks. Of course, you (or your partners) will also need some cash to close (down payment, closing costs, mandated property repairs, and perhaps, property improvements). If your balance sheet shows low amounts of cash (or near cash such as stocks, bonds, or CDs), consider selling some assets (cars, boats, vacation home, jewelry, and so on) to beef up your cash account. Liquidity not only adds to your credit capacity but also gives you the ready money to quickly jump on good deals when they arise.

How much residual income do you generate each month?   Many Americans spend and borrow so heavily that there's little if any money left over at the end of the month. Obviously, this type of month-to-month existence will seriously impede your ability to build wealth.

To boost your residual income, see what spending you can slash, what debts you can eliminate, and what luxuries (frivolities) you can do without. As financial planners emphasize, if you want to invest enough money to build wealth while you're still young enough to enjoy it, strictly discipline your spending and (unproductive) borrowing. Live well *below* your means.

Financial Goals   Now for the fun part. Given your financial resources and personal capabilities, how much money would you like to make over the next 5, 10, or 20 years? How many properties would you like to acquire? Do you plan to fix and flip, fix and hold, or merely buy and hold? Play around with some numbers. What looks doable? After you've worked through the numbers, commit a plan to

> **How much money do you want to make?**

writing. Attach a timetable. Set deadlines. Without a written plan, timetable, and goals, most people procrastinate. They drift. They regret. Avoid this perpetual trap. Commit yourself on paper and with action.

I realize that at this point we haven't yet discussed the types and sources of financial returns that are possible for entrepreneurial real estate investors. But after you have read and mastered the techniques of financial analysis, return to this part of the framework; then work through your possibilities. To reach your financial goals, you must first know what they are. With goals in mind, you must next map a path that will lead you to them.

Setting Up Your Analysis

As part of your effort to achieve superior profits and minimize risk, you should begin your evaluation of every property by addressing these issues:

- ◆ Identify the physical property.
- ◆ Identify the property rights that will come with ownership.
- ◆ Identify the area(s) that delineate the reasonable geographic boundaries for supply and demand.
- ◆ Set forth the time period of your analysis.

We will apply these topics in later chapters. At this point, you need to see why your investment analysis should explicitly consider each of these issues before you can accurately judge the merits of a proposed purchase.

Identify and Fully Describe the Physical Property

When you begin to compare income properties, your preliminary investigation should focus on identifying and describing each physical property in the following ways:

- Number and mix of the rental units
- Square footages of the total building and each rental unit
- Site size, boundaries, and amenities
- Type of construction, architectural style, and overall condition
- Personal property

In most mid-sized to large urban areas, small residential income properties come in a wide variety of sizes, shapes, styles, and conditions. You could run yourself ragged looking at everything that might become available. In addition, property price ranges, monthly rents, and vacancy rates will vary widely according to these prime physical characteristics. Securing these types of preliminary information can help you in two ways: It will help you narrow your search to only those properties that fall within your desired categories of investment, and it will guard you against comparing apples to oranges, which can inadvertently lead you into overpaying for a property or perhaps cause you to mistakenly pass up a bargain.

Number and Mix of Rental Units   Due to overall conditions of market supply and demand, various types of buildings and rental units experience different degrees of rental appeal. In some markets, a four-unit building that consists of all two-bedroom, two-bath units may rent much better than a four-unit building that includes all one-bedroom, one-bath units. Or say you face this choice: You can buy a 12-unit building that includes four efficiencies, four 2/1s, and four 1/1s, or you could buy a 16-unit property that consists of all 2/1s. Which is better?

> Not all income properties offer the same potential.

No absolute answer exists. It all depends on the nature of the local market. That's why your preliminary market analysis should try to identify the types of buildings and units that show the greatest tenant demand, lowest vacancies, and highest relative rent levels. I've seen beginning investors jump to buy say a 12-unit, supposedly bargain-priced building of 1/1s only to learn that the market was oversupplied with 1/1s. These investors then suffered more turnovers and higher vacancies than they had anticipated.

You will often see figures published on vacancy rates for the apartment "market." Never accept these figures at face value. On closer inspection, you will find that vacancy rates and tenant turnover do not hold constant across all types of properties, neighborhoods, and unit mixes. Talk with real estate agents, property managers, and other investors. Also, follow the listings of apartment rentals in the classified ads and the apartment rental services. Learn as much as you can about the widely diverse rental submarkets that actually combine to produce that market average.

> **Never rely on a so-called market vacancy rate.**

Square Footages   When you look at multi-unit properties, agents and owners will typically quote you two different types of square footage figures. One figure will apply to the total size of the building. The other type will apply to the sizes of the individual units. The naïve investor simply accepts these square footage figures at face value. The smart investor questions the figures more closely.

What floor areas are counted within the square footage figures?   Apartment buildings may devote space to hallways, basements, balconies, laundry facilities, and HVAC equipment as well as the actual living units themselves. Always break down total square footage figures and allocate them across the various types of building uses. A careful investigation requires this step for two important reasons.

First, no single standard applies to square footage measurements. Some owners or agents may count basements and balconies. Others may not. Again, precision helps you compare apples to apples. Second, you want to especially take note of *rentable* square footage. Some buildings waste a lot of square footage due to inefficient design. A building of 13,500 square feet might actually include more rentable square feet than another property that measures 15,000 square feet.

Owners and agents sometimes like to push their properties as a "great buy" because they compare favorably to the asking/sales prices of other properties on a price-per-square-foot basis. If the quality of that property's square footage stands inferior to its peer properties, however, it deserves to sell at a discounted price per square foot. The lower asking price does not signal the great buy the seller is claiming.

> **Not all square footage counts equally.**

Are the square footage figures accurate? Even though sellers and their agents nearly always disclaim their estimates of square footage, beginning investors still too often rely on the seller's figures only to learn later that those figures erred. In those instances where price per square foot counts heavily in your property comparisons and evaluations, pull out your tape measure. Check the relevant dimensions for yourself. That's the only way that you can protect yourself against the future shock of adverse surprise.

Are the rental units the right size? I've seen 2/2s as small as 600 or 700 square feet and as large as 1,300 or 1,400 square feet (not counting, of course, those premium-priced extravagant units found in luxury buildings in major cities and resort areas). Efficiencies may range in size from as small as 125 square feet up to 400 or 500 square feet. Other combinations of rooms and unit types can also show a wide variance in size.

To invest profitably, get a feel for the unit sizes that command the most appeal in your market. When a rental unit with the right combination of rooms still seems too small (or even too large), you will run into trouble keeping it rented without steeply discounting the rent level. Even with a rent discount, wrong-sized units will typically suffer greater tenant turnover.

Site Size and Features In many cities, the value of the land on which a building sits can easily total 30 to 70 percent of the property's total value. Even small differences in site size or features can add (or detract) tens of thousands of dollars vis-à-vis other seemingly similar properties.

> **Closely evaluate the size and quality of the site.**

I recently looked at two triplexes. Both properties brought in about the same amount of net income, yet one property was priced at $189,000 and the other was priced at $209,000. If you only considered the buildings themselves, the $189,000 property clearly looked like the better buy. But, in fact, the $209,000 property offered "hidden value" in the site. It turns out that this property's site size (and zoning) would permit a fourth unit to be built.

Additional site size also might prove valuable for adding on to a building, creating more parking or storage space, or providing better privacy. In evaluating a site, also take note of the quality of its landscaping and its egress and ingress (how easily cars can pull in and out of the property). Although uncommon in small income properties, on occasion you might find that a property includes a swimming pool, tennis courts, or other potentially desirable features and amenities.

When you're comparing various multi-unit investments, keep in mind that site size and features can significantly affect the value of the total property. Make sure you closely itemize all of those variations that can make a difference.

Type of Building   As you begin looking at small income properties, you will find all types of architectural styles, construction materials, and designs. These properties may also range in condition from pristine to borderline teardown. Some, too, are high maintenance. Others are low maintenance.

My first experiences.   When I first began buying apartments, I generally bought old, large, single-family houses that had been cut up and converted into multi-unit properties. Generally, these types of apartment buildings are priced at the low end of the market; they produce great cash flows, and because they may be difficult to finance through banks, their owners often offer seller financing.

> **Converted large houses can make great starter properties.**

On the downside, buildings of this type often suffer a high degree of functional and physical obsolescence. They're typically high maintenance, and they frequently lack individually controlled heat and air units. Nevertheless, for entry-level investors with limited cash or credit, I think this type of property can make a great starter investment.

Your experience. Depending on your resources and inclinations, such older properties may or may not appeal to you. But my basic point is to encourage you to get out into your market, look at properties, and compare prices, rent levels, cash flows, and managerial /maintenance requirements. You can then decide on the type of multi-unit property that best fits your investment profile. Just as Baskin-Robbins offers many flavors of ice cream, the real estate market offers many types of small income properties. Each type appeals to different tastes. Before you buy, inventory your choices. Evaluate the pros and cons of each type of property and the types of tenants that you would like to attract.

Personal Property   When you buy real estate, you're primarily paying for the land and the buildings. These items are called *real property;* however, part of a seller's asking price might also include *personal property,* which can include items such as laundry room equipment, refrigerators, stoves, and on occasion, furniture.

In addition, the price of the property could include items that are personal property by nature but have been so adapted for use with the building that the law classifies these items as *fixtures.* Fixtures typically include property such as ceiling fans, window air conditioning units, chandeliers, garage door openers, garbage disposals, built-in cabinets and bookshelves, and dishwashers.

Property evaluation. For purposes of property analysis and evaluation, you want to make sure that you fully understand not only the characteristics of the real property but also the precise description and listing of all personal property and fixtures that are to be included along with your purchase. Obviously (all other things equal), an apartment building where each unit is furnished with a washer, dryer, ceiling fans, range, dishwasher, and refrigerator is worth more than one that doesn't offer such items.

Source of mistakes.   Nevertheless, even though a property that includes a variety of personal property and fixtures is worth more than a similar property that lacks these items, the question still becomes, "How much more?" And the answer is, "Not as much as you might think." I will specifically address this issue with numbers when we get to the chapter on financial analysis. For now, keep in mind that differences among properties with respect to personal property and fixtures add another element to your investment analysis.

> **Never pay much for furniture and appliances.**

Understand Your Bundle of Rights and Restrictions

"This is *my* property! I'll do with it whatever I want to." Perhaps in long-ago times that predate zoning restrictions, building codes, tenants' rights, mortgages, written leases, and numerous other laws, ordinances, and contracts, such an uncompromised claim to ownership may have carried substantial weight. But not today.

Today, your rights to use, design, occupy, lease, mortgage, construct, add-on, or enjoy a property will likely be restricted in a dozen ways or more. As a smart investor, you will want to verify that your strategic plans for the properties you buy, manage, renovate, lease out, and sell comply with the legal rights that you actually possess. In general, your legal rights will be circumscribed by some or all of the following types of encumbrances.

> **Before you buy, verify what legal restrictions apply.**

Zoning In most cities, any property you buy will be located within a zoning district that is identified as, say, R-1A, R-4, C-2, or one of more than several dozen other types of districts. You can learn the applicable zoning district for any property by consulting your city or county's zoning map. After you learn the district classification for the property, you must next consult the rules and regulations portion of the written zoning ordinances. These rules will cover topics such as the following examples.

Use restrictions. Rules of use generally deal with basic questions of residential, commercial, professional, office, or industrial; however, these laws typically subdivide each of these major categories even more precisely. One residential zoning district might permit duplexes, where another will permit up to 24 units, and another might exclude all residential uses except single-family houses. Some zoning districts are called "exclusive," while others remain "inclusive." An inclusive commercial district might permit multi-unit residential, whereas an exclusive district would prohibit all uses except those that the law specifically lists.

Height and setbacks. As these terms imply, height restrictions limit the height of buildings (including roof signs and chimneys), and setback requirements tell property owners how closely they may legally build toward the front, side, and rear boundaries of a site. In addition to the building itself, setback distances may also apply to garages, decks, patios, paved parking areas, driveways, tennis courts, and swimming pools.

Height and setback requirements not only govern new construction but also limit what you can do to your property through renovations, conversions, and building additions. Before you buy a property with plans for improvement or additions (up or out), verify the legality of those changes. (Of course, this principle applies to all types of restrictions, not just height and setback rules.)

Occupancy. The zoning code's occupancy rules may limit the total number of persons who may live in a rental unit. In my city, for example, investors sometimes rent out their units to groups of four or five college students; however, in some single-family residential zoning districts, the law limits occupancy to three unrelated adults. Some communities also limit occupancy of rental units to two persons per bedroom.

When your market strategy aims for high-density occupancy, be aware that your plans may run counter to the law. Fortunately for investors, governments typically avoid enforcing occupancy laws unless they receive justifiable neighborhood complaints. Nevertheless, if you're thinking about buying a property that crowds tenants into the units (and thus greatly increases the cash flows from the amount of rent that otherwise could be obtained), check the legality of this strategy. If illegal, factor that risk into your purchase offer. If or when government seeks to enforce the code, you could see your gross rent collections plummet.

Architectural review boards.   Some communities may even regulate the color you paint a property or whether you can put up or take down shutters. Properties that are located in historical districts are especially susceptible to various architectural or "historical purity" regulations.

During a one-year period in San Francisco, the dictatorial architectural review board (ARB) received 12 renderings from developers who wanted to construct new high-rise projects in the city. The ARB rejected all of them on "aesthetic" grounds. On the positive side for existing investors, such rigorous standards for new construction and renovations does tend to reduce competition and keep rentals in short supply.

> **Coordinate a legal strategy with your market strategy.**

Lot size and building size.   Assume that you find a great vacant lot in an area zoned for quads. The economics look good for new construction and you're about to close the deal; then you discover a glitch. The size of the lot is too small—not too small to physically build the unit but too small for purposes of the zoning

code. Or say your study of the housing market shows a strong demand for efficiency apartments of about 350 square feet that
would easily rent at the very profitable rental rate of $450 per
month.

Alas, you find that zoning won't permit you to carry out this
market strategy. The law may require (quite absurdly, I might add)
that all residential rental units must contain a minimum of 500
square feet. Of course, if you built (or remodeled) to this larger size,
your costs would increase and you would have to charge a higher
rent. This low-end market segment of tenants who would prefer to
live alone is essentially forced into rental share arrangements because the code excludes small, less expensive rental units.

Again, I emphasize, when operating (building, managing, renovating) rental properties, your goal to find the most profitable
market strategy must always be tempered by the requirements of
the law. Absent compliance with every detail of the law, government regulators can force you to shelve your grand plans—even
when you've got ready tenants willing to pay for what you would
like to offer.

Building Codes   Ostensibly, building and construction codes at-
tempt to enhance the safety of buildings. To guarantee compliance,
cities and counties usually require major repairs, remodeling, and
renovations (as well as new construction) to pass through a government permitting process. Some property owners, though, try to
sidestep the permitting process, usually to save time, trouble, and
money. These owners hire unlicensed contractors or handymen to
complete their unpermitted, improvement projects.

Two implications.   As a potential investor and property owner,
this possibility of "bootlegged" work holds two implications: Never
buy a property that has been subject to unper-
mitted work without a substantial discount in
price, and when improving your own properties, always secure the necessary permits and inspections. Should you buy, own, or try to sell a

| Beware of |
| "bootlegged" work. |

property with nonconforming improvements, at some point when the inspectors do eventually discover the violations, they can force you to rip out the work and do it over in a manner that complies with the law.

Times have changed.   Years ago, the permit process and follow-up inspections were lax in many communities. Bootlegged work presented little risk of discovery. Today, however, and looking into the future, fewer and fewer officials are willing to turn a blind eye to code violations and unpermitted work. In addition, should non-conforming, unpermitted work cause or contribute to the injury or death of a tenant, you could face serious liability problems. Unless you like to tempt fate, make sure every property you buy or own complies with all building codes and other pertinent rules and regulations.

Environmental Laws   Investors in small income properties are most affected by environmental laws that relate to lead paint, asbestos, radon gas, and buried heating oil tanks. In addition, be wary of waste disposal (sewage) systems that aren't connected to a municipal sewage line. You may think that in this modern era, no urban properties would lack sewer connections. Unfortunately, that's not the case. For example, Sarasota County, Florida, is one of the wealthiest urban areas in the United States, yet tens of thousands of properties in that county (even some on major thoroughfares) remain without a modern sewer system.

For a complete rundown of the environmental issues that may apply in the areas where you plan to invest, consult your state or local environmental protection agencies for their informative brochures. Also, the U.S. Department of Housing and Urban Development (www.hud.gov) publishes a variety of brochures that discuss environmental issues of interest to owners of residential properties.

Lease Terms   When you buy a property that is currently occupied by tenants, you must continue to honor the terms of those

> **Read the tenants' leases before you buy.**

leases into which the previous seller entered. Do you plan to increase rents? Do you plan to make renovations? Do you plan to move into that choice corner unit with gorgeous views of both the bay and the mountains?

If your tenants' existing leases give them rights that conflict with your plans, you must put your plans on hold until those leases expire.[5] That's why you must secure and read copies of every lease that applies to the units in the buildings that you are buying. Who knows? Unless you read the leases, you may learn too late that the seller has given his brother a written five-year lease on the best unit in the building at a rent level that's half the market rate.

Tenants Rights Laws   In addition to closely reading the existing leases, you will also want to check with regulators or an attorney to learn whether your tenants-to-be are covered by any type of tenant rights laws. Such laws might pertain to rent increases, mandated repairs, condominium conversions, evictions, or security deposits. Generally, when a lease conflicts with a tenants' rights statute (or a court decision), the law stands supreme.

The spread of consumerism.   Increasingly, with our society's shift to so-called consumer protection laws, state and local governments are setting more and more rules to govern investor-tenant relations. Except in those cities where ultraliberal politics reign, tenants' rights laws will not materially affect your rental operations. Nevertheless, you must follow the technicalities of these laws to a tee; otherwise, you can open yourself up to some onerous penalties.

Tenants' rights can hurt those who are their intended beneficiaries.   For a horror story of tenants rights, watch the video

---

5. As an alternative, you could try to negotiate with the tenants to modify the terms of the lease. Some investors even pay the existing tenants to vacate earlier than the lease stipulates.

movie *Pacific Heights* starring Michael Keaton as the evil tenant who knows how to play the housing court system for all it's worth. On the bright side, had the owners of the Pacific Heights property featured in the movie continued to own that building through 2002, they would have seen it more than quadruple in value during the 15 years since the movie *Pacific Heights* was filmed.

> **Before you buy, rent the video *Pacific Heights*.**

In a narrow sense, lopsided tenants rights laws seem to favor tenants. Over the longer run, such laws discourage new housing supply and thus drive down vacancies, push up property prices, and make life miserable for all persons who would like reasonable accommodations at an affordable price, either through rental or purchase. High rent levels and property prices now prohibit nearly all of the middle class from living in San Francisco. Most property investors, though, have made millions.

> **Left-wing politics creates real estate millionaires.**

Fair Housing Laws Undoubtedly you are aware that various federal, state, and local laws outlaw certain types of discrimination. If you own a 12-unit apartment building, neither you nor your manager could refuse to rent to tenants because of their sex, race, religion, color, ethnicity, disability, or children (unless you own a property that fits within the age-55-or-over exception).

However, some states and cities (and courts) have expanded the categories of protected tenants to include, for example, homosexuals, cohabiting couples of the opposite sex, college students, and members of the military. To learn the precise fair housing laws that will apply to your properties, consult an attorney or your local fair housing office.

Also, be aware that fair housing laws frequently exempt certain types of properties such as single-family houses, roommate shares, and two- to four-unit, owner-occupied buildings. When it comes to compliance with fair housing laws, property owners must tread carefully. Violations (and especially a longstanding pattern of illegal practices) could easily cost you your life savings.

Take no chances here. Learn the law and then follow it scrupulously.

Mortgages   You know that if you fail to pay your mortgage, your lender can push you into foreclosure. Unless you pay the full amount you owe, you will lose all of your rights of ownership, use, and occupancy. However, relatively few people know that your mortgage contract limits your property rights in several other important ways.

Owner occupancy.   Mortgage lenders give their most favorable loan terms and lowest interest rates to those borrowers who live in the property that they are financing. That's why I encourage first-time (or cash-short) investors to buy a two- to four-unit property. If you agree to live in one of the units for at least a year, you can finance the deal with a down payment of just 3 to 5 percent.

> **Buy a quad.**
>
> **Live in one unit.**

Even so, never lie about your intent to occupy a rental property so that you can qualify for easier and lower-cost financing. Some investors pull this trick, but they don't realize that this deceit exposes them not only to a foreclosure but also to a felony conviction with heavy fines and an extended stay in federal prison. When you tell a lender that you will live in a property (absent a truly unexpected and serious change of circumstances), you are legally and contractually bound to abide by that commitment.

Property alterations.   Many mortgages include a clause that reads something similar to the following:

> Borrower shall maintain the property in good repair and shall make no material alterations without the written consent of the lender.

This requirement can affect investors in two ways. It limits your God-given right to become a slumlord. If you bleed a property to the extent that it becomes run down, the lender could declare the mortgage immediately due and payable. If you fail to pay off the loan as demanded, the lender could foreclose.

Also, this clause requires you to notify the lender and seek permission before you undertake any extensive renovations, re-modeling, or additional construction. You might wonder, "Why should the lender care? Surely, if I improve the property, the lender's position becomes more secure because I'm increasing the value of the property." Unfortunately, on occasion, your sup-position proves false.

> **Consult your lender before you renovate.**

I can testify from years of inspecting and evaluating properties that not all owner-designed "improvements" create value. Time and time again, I've looked at a remodeled property and just been amazed. As I stare at some bastardized renovation, I ask myself or the real estate agent, "What in the world was this guy thinking?" I guarantee you that too many owners fail to test their personal tastes and creative ideas against the opinion of the marketplace. (Of course, you won't make this mistake because you will thor-oughly research tenant preferences before you begin your im-provements.)

Easements   Through an easement, one party obtains the right to use the property of someone else for a specified purpose. For ex-ample, owners of beachfront properties may have to grant the public an access route through their land. Utility companies often secure easements to erect and maintain electrical lines or water pipes. In cases where one building lot without street access is split off from another street-fronting lot, the owners of the back lot may gain a driveway easement through the front lot so that they can ac-cess their property.

As an investor, you must clearly identify any easements that may restrict your right to use or improve any properties you plan to buy. On other occasions, as the purchaser of a property, you may obtain easement rights to use or pass through the property of someone else. Either way, easements (or the lack thereof) can ma-

> **Easements may add or subtract from property value.**

terially affect the value and usability of property. Make sure you fully understand the precise nature of any easements that apply to your real estate investments.

Homeowner Associations and Deed Restrictions   In addition to all of the rules and regulations of government, many property owners must also comply with a myriad of homeowner association restrictions. Such rules are typically drafted by the elected officers of the association. In addition, some rules of usage also "run with the land." This phrase means that the rules are actually recorded in the deed to the property that is located in the county (parish) courthouse.

Although homeowner association rules and deed restrictions most commonly apply to condominiums, townhouses, and single-family houses, such restrictions may also apply to small income properties. I am currently negotiating the purchase of a triplex on Siesta Key (Florida) that is actually part of a condominium association of just four properties (all triplexes). Some of the pertinent restrictions for this property are shown in Figure 2.2.

Property Rights: Summing Up   We began this discussion of property rights with the once often-heard boast, "It's my property. I'll do with it as I please." As a smart investor, you can now see that such an assertion sounds foolhardy.

To avoid errors and unpleasant surprises, take nothing for granted. Before you buy, investigate everything from A to Z—from association rules to zoning. Many property owners have created great strategic plans for their sites and buildings only to later learn that such plans violate some law, rule, regulation, or contract restriction. It's true that you *will* profit most when you tailor your physical property and managerial operations toward a well-chosen market segment of tenants, but it's also true that to earn those profits, you cannot charge ahead with your eyes closed.

Those rules that are specifically set forth in the Declaration, By-Laws, or Articles of Incorporation as amended or that have been adopted by the Board of Directors will be strictly enforced. Your reading of these rules and your voluntary compliance with them will facilitate the proper management of this condominium and promote the best interests of all unit owners.

I. *ANIMALS OR PETS*
1. Only one (1) cat, bird, or small dog (under 15 pound) may be kept in a unit. The occupant will be responsible to repair all damage done by a pet and will indemnify and hold the Association and the Board of Directors harmless against all claims for injuries to persons or damage to property caused by their pet.
2. Pets are the responsibility of their owners and shall not become a nuisance or disturbance of any kind to others. Alpino Bioanco Villas has always had a leash rule. Pets are not permitted on Condominium property unless accompanied by their owner. Pets may NOT be tied outside the unit and left unattended, nor will they be permitted to roam. OWNERS MUST CLEAN UP AFTER THEIR PETS. OTHERWISE, OWNERS WILL BE FINED AND IF VIOLATIONS CONTINUE, THE PET WILL BE DECLARED A NUISANCE AND REMOVED FROM THE COMPLEX.
3. All pets must be registered with the Association office.

II. *VEHICLES AND PARKING*
Each unit shall be assigned one (1) regular parking space for a passenger automobile. The remaining four (4) parking spaces are reserved for guests and business and visitors. All vehicles to be regularly parked must be registered with the Manager. No trucks, commercial vans, pickups, lettered vehicles, motor homes, or travel trailers may be parked on the Condominium property except temporarily while servicing a unit, loading or unloading. Any longer period than overnight is prohibited. No boats or boat trailer may be parked on Condominium property at any time.

Abandoned vehicles will be towed away at the owner's expense. All parking spaces shall be kept clear of refuse, parts, equipment or other materials.

Bicycles, mopeds, motorcycles, and similar vehicles may be stored in designated storage areas under the buildings at the risk of the owner.

Figure 2.2   Sample Triplex Condominium Rules and Regulations.

III. *USE OF OUTSIDE PORCHES AND STAIRWAYS*

Second-floor occupants may not use the porches or railings for airing bedding, drying clothing or other materials. Barbecue grills or equipment may be used only on ground-floor grass or concrete areas, not on balconies due to fire hazard. All loose and moveable objects should be removed during severe windstorms.

IV. *GARBAGE AND TRASH*

All garbage, trash, and refuse must be placed in plastic bags, taped or tied at the top, and placed in garbage receptacles. No junk, inflammable materials, or discarded materials may be allowed to accumulate, and each unit and the common areas shall at all times be kept in a clean and sanitary condition. Occupants shall not allow anything to fall or be thrown from second-floor windows, doors, or balconies.

V. *STORAGE ROOMS*

Storage rooms may be used for storage of household goods, hobby materials, and equipment, but all risk of loss or damage shall be assumed by the owner of such materials. No activity shall be conducted in the storage rooms that would constitute a fire or health hazard, increase insurance rates, or create a nuisance to the other occupants of the Condominium property.

VI. *NOISE*

Radios, recording amplifiers, and television sets must be turned to a minimum volume between the hours of 11:00 P.M. and 8:00 A.M.

VII. *OCCUPANCY*

No unit may be occupied on a regular basis by more than two persons per bedroom. This rule shall not apply to occasional visits by houseguests. No occupant shall make use of any unit that violates any laws, ordinances, or regulations of any governmental body, the Condominium documents, or these House Rules.

VIII. *MISCELLANEOUS*

Under no circumstances may a unit be occupied by a minor without supervision of a responsible adult.

Figure 2.2   *(Continued)*

This caution especially applies at the time you're negotiating price. Without clear knowledge of pertinent restrictions, you may overestimate the profit possibilities. Unwarranted optimism can entice you into paying too much for a property, or perhaps borrowing more than the property's realistic cash flows can cover. As you will see, in today's investment climate, the highest returns are earned by those entrepreneurial investors who can turn an underperforming property into a winner. But your acts of magic can't succeed against impermissible change.

Where Should You Invest?

For convenience, most investors who own single-family rental houses limit their search for properties to a geographic area that falls within a 30- to 60-minute radius of their personal residence. Typically, such investors want to remain close to their properties so that they can easily deal with day-to-day issues (showing the property, making repairs, disciplining tenants, and so on). As an owner of small income properties, especially as you gain experience and trade up to larger properties, you need not follow such a constrained acquisition strategy. With income properties, you can delegate those day-to-day tasks to your on-site manager.

Ideally, you want to invest in those geographic areas that will provide the best economic climate and the highest property appreciation. Before you choose a location for your investments, investigate its local job picture. You will want to assess its potential for growth in population and new development of competing properties. During the next decade or two, real estate investors in some areas of the country will enjoy a doubling, tripling, or even quadrupling of their property values and rent levels, whereas property owners in other locales may do well to merely keep up with inflation.

To the extent possible, invest for growth. That's why unlike most books that deal with investing in real estate, this book helps you identify those areas that show the most promise for strong economic performance and avoid areas that present higher risk and lagging economic prospects.

Before you even think about choosing a specific property, discover where the local economy is headed. When possible, climb aboard a boat that's sailing into a rising tide. You can't expect your properties to show strong appreciation when they're anchored in a sea that's receding. As I describe in Chapter 3, I learned this lesson the hard way.

Time Period

As part of your investment strategy, think about the length of time you plan to hold each of your acquisitions. If you plan to fix and flip, your economic and market analysis need not look out any further than 6 to 12 months. On the other hand, as a buy, improve, and hold investor, you would want to take a mid- to long-range perspective of, say, 5 to 20 years.

Different time perspectives can lead to substantially different investment choices. Right now, for example, I believe that many lower-priced neighborhoods and communities throughout the United States are poised for turnaround and dramatic property appreciation; however, to successfully invest in these areas requires a patient investor. If you want to earn quick cash, you could focus primarily on trying to find bargain-priced properties that you can fix up and immediately resell (or exchange). In any case, don't choose your locations or your properties until after you've clearly thought through the how and the when of your exit strategy.

> **Plan your exit strategy.**

CHAPTER 3

Where's the Local Economy Headed?

During the late 1980s, an acquaintance of mine (whom I will call Tom) was fixing and flipping $500,000 properties in Contra Costa County, about 15 miles east of San Francisco. Tom was making a killing ($50,000 to $75,000 per house). He had been working one house at a time (three- to six-month holding period), but the money was rolling in so fast that he decided to leverage up. In 1989, Tom borrowed heavily, quit his day job, and bought three more houses simultaneously. He decided that because the fix and flip business was the next best thing to printing money, he would do it full time.

Before Tom could fix up and liquidate his current three-house inventory, however, the local economy turned against him. Still, Tom plowed ahead. He had succeeded in the past, he told himself, and he would succeed now. Besides, the recession would probably blow over in a matter of months. It didn't. And within a year Tom was upside down on all three properties. Even after renovations, the houses were worth less than when he had bought them. What's worse, he had depleted his cash to pay for the property improvements and his out-of-pocket carry for principal, interest, taxes, insurance (PITI) on the acquisition loans totaled $12,774 per month.

> **Learn the facts about your local economy.**

Needless to say, this fellow was suffering a world of hurt. Tom's hard-earned profits of the preceding four years were evaporating. Although I would like to report a happy ending, it didn't happen. Tom did put tenants in each of the properties to partly stem the hemorrhaging from negative cash flows, but his rent collections amounted to only $5,250 per month. His three alligators were still chewing him up. Plus, his family's household budget required another $7,000 a month (out of which $4,100 went to cover the PITI on his home mortgage). Tom hung on for another two years, but eventually the crushing burden of debt forced him to sell. In the end, his total capital and carrying losses on those three properties exceeded $400,000.

Four Lessons

Sad to say, during the early-to-mid 1990s, Tom's setback had many counterparts. In Los Angeles, Houston, Dallas, Boston, and New York City, many similarly unwise investors were spun upside down.

What can you learn from their misfortunes? Here are four lessons:

1. Never pursue an investment strategy in real estate without closely monitoring the local economy and local real estate market where you are investing.
2. Beware of using more leverage (debt) than you can safely handle; correspondingly, don't let those alluring high dollar returns spellbind you into growing too fast or taking on too many properties at the same time.
3. Plan multiple market strategies. Even boom economies can go bust within a period of 6–12 months—or perhaps we should say, *especially* boom economies can turn to bust relatively quickly.
4. Don't quit your day job prematurely. (Trust me on this one. I, too, at one giddy time abandoned good sense in

favor of what I unrealistically figured would be quick and easy profits. And like Tom, I had not considered or prepared for a downside contingency.[1])

Although we shall discuss each of these four lessons in due course, in this chapter, I primarily show you how and why to judge the strength and direction of a local economy.

Economic Base Matters Greatly

"The author did it—and so can you!" So opens the blurb page of the classic bestseller, *How I Turned $1,000 into a Million in My Spare Time,* by William Nickerson (Pocket Books, 1962). With these words of encouragement, I devoured the contents of this book. And at age 21, I began to immediately put this author's advice into practice. I soon found what I thought were super bargains. According to Nickerson's formula, the price of an income property should equal 10 times the property's net operating income (NOI). Using this formula, I couldn't believe the fantastic deals

> **Income multiples relate to growth expectations.**

that were coming my way. I routinely bought small apartment buildings for five to seven times NOI. In other words, I bought income properties that according to Nickerson's advice should have sold for $100,000. Yet, I paid only $50,000 to $70,000.[2] I thought to myself, these sellers are crazy. They don't know what they're doing.

Alamo, California (San Francisco Bay Area) versus Terre Haute, Indiana

As it turned out, it was I who erred. I failed to understand that I should not have applied Nickerson's pricing formula in my own

---

1. This business deal did not pertain to real estate.

2. These figures reflect proportionality, not the actual numbers.

home town. Unlike Alamo, California (where Nickerson lived), my home town of Terre Haute, Indiana suffered a stagnant local economy and a shrinking population. Whereas Nickerson's properties typically doubled in value over a period of 10 years, mine (even after improvements) struggled to keep pace with inflation. Fortunately, these properties did yield huge amounts of positive cash flow; and because these beginning investment experiences predated 1986 Tax Reform Act (TRA), they also provided huge amounts of tax write-offs. Using this tax shelter, I enjoyed virtually tax-free income from both my property rent collections and my professional earnings.

Authors Neglect Economic Base

Why did I fail to realize the importance of economic base? Because Nickerson, like most of the other authors who have penned bestselling books on real estate investing, neglected to tell his readers how to evaluate their local economies. Robert Allen merely says, "Homes and apartment buildings will always be in demand, regardless of what the economy may do. People must live somewhere; they have no choice. Housing is a basic need."[3]

> **Leading gurus erroneously ignore economic base.**

Or, more recently, consider Kevin Meyers: "[Fixing and flipping], in many respects, is a recession-proof business. Regardless of the external economy, people need and want quality housing and will pay top dollar . . . ."[4] Likewise, the authors of the similar "get rich in real estate" books completely ignore the fact that smart real estate investors need to study a city's economic base prior to shaping their investment strategy. Without a growing local economy, demand for rentals will typically sag. With a growing local economy, your potential tenants will multiply in number and their pay-

3. Robert Allen, *Nothing Down* (New York: Simon & Schuster, 1980), 22.

4. Kevin Meyers, *Buy It, Fix It, Sell It, Profit!* (Chicago: Dearborn, 1998), 2.

checks will continuously show increasing earnings. The economic pie serves up bigger slices for nearly everyone.

Benefit from the Lessons Learned

Some local areas stagnate. Some move slowly ahead on an even keel. Some markets swing wildly from boom to bust and then from bust to boom. Some historically stable areas are posed for boom. Others will enter gradual decline.

One key to long-term success lies with the ability to anticipate and prepare. Batten down hatches during pending storms. (By the mid-1980s, for example, I saw the ominous signs of overbuilding and increasing unemployment in Dallas, Texas. I then liquidated my Dallas rental properties near the top of the market.) Conversely, you should increase your property holdings in cities or neighborhoods where prices do not yet incorporate the area's true potential for growth.

Even when you plan to fix and flip rather than improve and hold, don't set yourself up to get whipsawed (as my friend Tom did) by high debt and softening prices. If the economic signals in your area flash yellow, slow down. Temper your ambitions. Increase your cash position. Closely monitor any cracks in your investment and market strategies. Create alternatives. Just as important, move quickly when the signals look promising. You are about to profit big from the next cyclical upswing.

> **Profit from market bottoms.**

Although the precise economic signals for which to watch vary by time and place, as a guide, pay attention to those on the following list:

I.   Demand: Evaluate consumer buying power
    A.   Population growth
    B.   Employment and incomes
    C.   Costs of doing business

        D.   Quality of life
        E.   Wealth
        F.   Community attitudes
        G.   Entrepreneurial spirit

II.   Supply: Evaluate your potential competition
        A.   New construction
        B.   Existing homes for sale
        C.   Existing homes for rent
        D.   Condos for sale
        E.   Condos for rent
        F.   Apartment vacancy rates
        G.   Apartment rent levels
        H.   Available buildable land
        I.   Delinquencies and mortgage foreclosures

As a beginning investor, you may want to dispense with all of this talk about economic base, market signals, demand, and supply. "Just tell me what I need to know to make a lot of money," you say. But that's precisely the point. Until you check the facts about your local economy or the local economy where you plan to invest, you're shooting blind. You may hit your target, but then again, you may not. Even when you score a sequence of hits, don't get too cocky (as we all are prone to do). While you're basking in glory, someone just might move the target.

Where to Get Data

You don't need to become an economist or full-fledged market researcher to uncover these population and economic data. Your

> **Rely on your local resources.**

local Realtor, mortgage lender, and homebuilder associations regularly collect and often publish these data and similarly useful statistics. Other data sources include utility companies, the economic research bureau of your local college or the state university, and your local or regional urban planning office.

Will the Population Grow?

Essentially, population growth (or lack thereof) results from three sources: births, mortality, and people moving into or out of an area. Try to get a good overview about your area. Look at the sources of growth or decline. Are more people moving in, or moving away? How is the age distribution of the population changing?

Most people think of Florida as Heaven's waiting room, but in fact, the number of children in the state is growing quickly. Even if the number of seniors flooding into the state should slow (which I certainly do not expect), a long line of children will provide a consistent and increasing demand for rental apartments and houses.

Pockets of Existing and Potential Growth

Look for emerging areas.

Population growth seldom spreads itself evenly across a city or metro area. Geographic areas develop pockets or corridors of growth. Try to determine where the heaviest growth has occurred. Is this area reaching its limit? Are the roads and freeways choked with traffic? Have rents and housing prices shot upwards? Where will the next burst of population increase occur?

Find Out the Actual Numbers

The media often reports that the population growth *rate* of an area is slowing down. Most people interpret this statement to mean that growth *itself* is slowing. Quite often that's not the case. Rather, as the population base of an area gets larger, the percentage increase can fall even though the number of people moving in continues to increase.

Say that during the 1990s the population of a county jumped from 300,000 to 400,000; therefore, the decade brought an overall growth rate of 33 percent. During the 2000s, this overall growth rate is expected to fall to 25 percent. Nevertheless, even with this lower growth rate, the county population will increase by 100,000, exactly the same *number* of people as in the previous decade. It is the *number* of people who create demand, not the growth rate *per se.* Watch the numbers.

Beware of False Negatives

If you look at the population growth figures for Highland Park, Texas, Washington, D.C., or New York City, you would see very little

Evaluate big picture influences on smaller areas.

upward movement during the past 30 years. Yet, housing prices and rent levels in each of these cities have climbed to rank among the highest in the United States. Why? Because these cities draw their demand from their much larger surrounding metro areas. To judge the total demand for housing in a specific community or neighborhood, tally up the projected population growth figures for entire contiguous areas. Focus on too small an area and you'll miss the big picture.

Is the Number of Jobs Increasing?

To grow and prosper, most (but not all) areas need a core of *basic* employment. Essentially, you want to identify an area's major employers, the predominant types of businesses, their potential for growth, and, on the downside, whether any cutbacks, layoffs, or closings seem imminent.

Specifically, basic employers bring money into an area. When these businesses decline, so do all of the non-basic businesses that feed off the revenues generated by these core firms (or government agencies and institutions). For example, basic employers typically include the following:

1. **Manufacturers.** To see the critical role that manufacturers play, watch the Michael Moore movie, *Roger and Me.* This documentary catalogues the economic downfall of Flint, Michigan, after General Motors closed the local Buick factory.

2. **Professional service firms.** Most low- and mid-level architects, lawyers, accountants, consultants, and advertising agencies count only as town fillers, not town builders. Similarly classified are real estate agents, stock brokers, and insurance agencies; however, some professional (or financial) service firms cater to a regional, statewide, national, or even global clientele. The billings of these firms may bring millions—even billions—of dollars into a local economy.

3. **Medical services.** Health care has become the largest business in the United States, and undoubtedly will become much larger as the baby boomers begin to hit their 60s. Many local areas are now maintaining hospitals, clinics, and testing labs that bring in patients from hundreds (or even thousands) of miles away. Think Mayo Clinic.

4. **Travel and tourism.** It seems as though nearly every urban and rural area in the country now wants to capture part of the more than $250 billion a year that Americans spend on travel, tourism, conventions, and other leisure-related activities. Think McCormick Place or the Jacob Javits Center.

5. **Colleges and universities.** Many towns and cities house one or more colleges or universities that bring millions (or billions) into the local area. Boston, for example, is home to 62 colleges. In this sense, education truly does pay.

6. **Retailing/Distribution.** The Omni shopping center in Miami attracts shoppers who live in Mexico, Brazil, and Argentina. Honey Creek Mall in Terre Haute draws in shoppers from the surrounding rural areas and small

towns up to 60 miles away. Neighborhood 7–11s contribute little to an area's economic base, but large malls, catalogue centers, and warehousing operations (such as Amazon.com, L.L. Bean) can employ hundreds or even thousands based on revenues derived from throughout the region, country, or the world.

7. **Centers of government.** Obviously, cities that house the state (provincial) capitols receive enormous tax revenues from the residents of their respective jurisdictions, just as Washington, D.C. (Ottawa) receive in tax dollars from throughout the United States (Canada). In addition, many other cities derive revenues from the state and federal agencies, military bases, defense contractors, and Veteran's Administration hospitals located in the area. Think NASA and Titusville, Florida.

Amazingly, very few small investors pay much attention to their area's basic employment—unless their economy has already turned into recession. When the Southern California economy boomed in the late 1980s, real estate investors and homebuyers alike thought those 10 to 20 percent a year property appreciation rates would last forever. When the Berlin Wall fell in 1989, few property owners or potential buyers could see any implications for San Diego home prices and apartment rents.

> **Look for areas of job growth. Anticipate slowdowns.**

What Was the San Diego Connection?

Defense spending. Defense contractors provided a significant percentage of the basic jobs in Southern California. After the Berlin Wall fell, Congress, quite predictably, slashed defense spending. Defense contractors, in turn, slashed tens of thousands of jobs. In addition, Congress severely cut back the number of personnel stationed at the San Diego Naval Base.

As unemployment went up, housing demand and housing prices (rent levels) fell. Nearly everyone connected with home-building and home selling began to feel the effects. Homebuilders shut down their construction sites. Most real estate agents, home inspectors, property lawyers, title insurers, and apartment managers experienced cuts in income. These depressing effects further rippled through the local economy.

Forecasting Recovery

At that time, I was living in Berkeley, California, and frequently flew down to San Diego (La Jolla) for weekend excursions. I kept my eye on market signals firsthand. By the mid-1990s, everything was in place. The market bottom was clear. Both population and job growth were moving up. Mortgage lenders were making it easier to borrow. That's when I wrote, "By the year 2001, many renters throughout Southern California will sorely regret the housing bargains they missed during the mid 1990s.[5]

Yet, as of 1996, the so-called real estate expert for the *San Francisco Examiner* wrote, "A home is where the bad investment is" (November 17, 1996). And another California expert wrote, "The quick buck profits [in real estate] are long gone. . . . Buying a property in excellent condition and hoping somehow to earn a profit is a no-win situation" (*San Diego Union-Tribune,* September 8, 1996).

Why did I see what others missed? Because I know how to read and weigh market signals. And that's the talent that I would like you to learn. Most people merely extend the present or recent past into the future. That's why several years back the stock enthusiasts all forecasted stock market gains of 10 to 15 percent annually. (Do you recall the bestselling books, *Dow 36,000,* Times Books, 1999, and *Stocks for the Long Run,* 2nd edition McGraw-Hill, 1998?)

> **Profit from reading market signals.**

---

5. Gary W. Eldred, *Stop Renting Now* (NIHO, 1996), 161.

Neither I nor anyone else can *precisely* forecast when and by how much home prices or rents will increase or decrease; however, you need not aim for such *precision*. Your goal is to monitor fundamentals and then temper your strategy accordingly.

Robert Schiller (*Irrational Exuberance,* Princeton University, 2000) began his critique of the stock hypesters in November, 1996. Even then, stock prices were out of whack with earnings and dividends. Yet, the major stock indexes continued to shoot up until early 2000. Nevertheless, by 2003, those investors who had heeded Schiller's warnings in 1997 or 1998 (and moved their money into bonds or real estate) were far ahead of those investors who refused to change their investment strategy.

Cost of Running a Business

Why did the old-time New England textile manufacturers move their factories to the South? Why did many Silicon Valley technology firms move all or part of their operations to Austin, Texas? Why did my publisher, John Wiley & Sons, Inc., recently give up its long-time world headquarters at 605 3rd Avenue, New York City, in favor of a new office complex just across the Hudson River in Hoboken, New Jersey? Why do business analysts forecast huge growth in warehousing and distribution employment along the I-4 corridor that links Daytona Beach, Orlando, and Tampa-St. Petersburg? Costs. Lower costs of running a business.

Businesses and Employment Migrate to Lower-Cost Cities, States, and Countries

In the highly competitive, national and global marketplace, major firms persistently scout for business locations that will reduce their costs of labor, transportation, real estate, energy, and taxes. In addition, they look to see what kinds of incentives that government(s) might provide such as worker training, low-interest financing, and tax abatements.

At times, this search may simply encourage a move from the central business core to the suburbs, or perhaps across state lines to a more tax-friendly environment. On other occasions, the move may take the firm's jobs to a different state or country. Overall, you need to size up the relative cost competitiveness of the area(s) where you plan to invest. Do you think that its cost structure (on balance) will encourage employers to move in—or push them to move out?

> **Look for areas that attract new businesses.**

Cost of Living for Employees

Firms also factor in an area's costs of living for employees. The quip in Silicon Valley for the past several years has been, "What do you call a techie who earns $150,000 a year?" Answer: A renter. Given the outrageously high living costs (especially housing prices, but also California state income taxes, traffic congestion, and auto and homeowner's insurance), many Silicon Valley firms will need to find alternative locations that provide a more affordable lifestyle for employees.

In the past, Salt Lake City, Seattle, and Austin were able to capitalize on the fact that they gave employees lower living costs. While still true to a degree (relative to the San Francisco Bay Area and Silicon Valley), these cities can no longer offer the clear cut advantages they displayed at the start of the 1990s. The question now becomes: Where are the next hot spots for tech (or other types of employment) that will grow strongly in the future?

Quality of Life (QOL)

Today, more and more people are choosing the places where they will work for the quality of life as well as the money rewards. Executives evaluate new locations on the basis of climate, recreational amenities, school systems, cultural facilities, municipal services, crime rates, housing costs, and traffic congestion.

Many communities that seek growth try to build their quality of life images. A passage from an Edmonton, Alberta, economic brochure reads as follows:

> The distinct seasons enjoyed by Edmontonians are indicative of the recreational activities available. Summers are warm, with daytime temperatures averaging 22°C (72°F) and evening temperatures cooling to a pleasant 15°C (60°F). Summer is complemented by a mild spring and autumn, as well as plenty of sunshine, making much of the year enjoyable for hiking, cycling, trail riding, golf, tennis, and camping. Bicycle and hiking trails in the city's Capital City Park are linked by four pedestrian footbridges across the North Saskatchewan River. Along this river valley are adjacent golf courses, boat launches, picnic sites, and a beautiful network of trails. Winters are characterized by clear blue skies, low humidity, and very little wind. The coldest month is January, the average high being –10°C (16°F) and the average low being –18°C (0°F). With crisp winter temperatures and an average annual snowfall of 140 cm (55″), Edmonton is an ideal city for winter sport enthusiasts. In the winter, the hiking trails are converted to accommodate snow-shoeing and cross-country skiing. In addition to the river trails, many other fine cross-country ski trails and downhill facilities are located within, or in close proximity to, Edmonton.
>
> To complement the pleasant summers and invigorating winters, Edmonton offers virtually pollution-free and pollen-free air.
>
> Edmonton is a city to be enjoyed by all, for all seasons.

Does that picture arouse your desire to seek a job or start a business in Edmonton? The city leaders hope so, for during the coming years the cities that achieve economic growth will be

> **Invest in areas with high QOL.**

those that can sell their advantages as a good place to raise a family and enjoy life. How does your area rate? What serious efforts, if any, are being made to improve it?

Quality of Life Also Attracts Wealth

Survey the people who have bought property in Aspen, Colorado; Jackson Hole, Wyoming; Longboat Key, Florida; Banner Elk, North Carolina; Ashland, Oregon; or Sedona, Arizona. To a great degree, they're not the people who currently hold jobs in those areas. Rather, they're people with relatively high incomes or wealth who choose where they want to live or maintain a second home. Many high income free agents such as writers, consultants, inventors, and entrepreneurs also enjoy both the money and occupational freedom to live wherever they want.

Those cities, towns, and rural areas that can appeal to the footloose and financially mobile will continue to experience high demand for their residential properties. With no doubts whatsoever, this trend will continue. As boomers head into retirement, as the Internet (and intranet) revolution permits increasing numbers of people to work from home—no matter where that home is located—people will abandon high-cost, low-quality-of-life areas in favor of those locations where they would truly prefer to live. Will your area attract these folks?

> **Where will boomers migrate?**

Community Attitudes and Actions

Another factor that boosts demand and explains why some areas grow faster than others is community attitudes. Specifically, do the city leaders want economic growth?

In some states and cities, the answer to this question is "no." Sometimes local business or government leaders discourage new firms from locating in an area as a way to protect vested interests. Sometimes local politicians develop a power base that they do not want outsiders to challenge. The local citizenry may want to preserve a way of life.[6] Through elected and appointed officials, they make it difficult for new firms to obtain permits, licenses, and zoning approval.[7] In the past—and especially in towns dominated by one or at most several major employers—powerful owners of existing firms have successfully kept new industry out of an area. Their chief reason has been to avoid additional bidders for available workers and thereby maintain low-wage rates.

In cities that want economic growth, however, firms and private organizations, as well as various government officials, actively recruit investment and new employers. For example, the Jacksonville, Florida, Chamber of Commerce hired a national consulting firm to prepare a comprehensive economic analysis of that city. One purpose of the study was to identify the types of employers whose needs would best match Jacksonville's strengths. In addition, the consultant recommended ways that Jacksonville community leaders could improve the marketing of the city to targeted employers. Similarly, two of the rapidly growing areas in North America have been Calgary and Edmonton, Alberta, Canada. Although their economies benefited from the well-endowed resource base of Alberta (especially oil), a contributing factor has also been the pro-business, pro-growth attitude of the provincial and city governments. In Canada, a country where left-leaning political attitudes tend to dominate, Alberta has gained a reputation for free enterprise.

---

6. During the late 1970s, Oregon opposed economic growth quite loudly, even to the extent of advertising Oregon as a state where newcomers were not welcome. By 1984, though, political leaders and citizens had changed their tune. Badly hurt by the recession of 1981–82 and still slow to recover, Oregon went out to recruit new industry.

7. Recently, the city fathers in Terre Haute turned away 400 high-paying jobs because local power brokers opposed the company (a major chemical manufacturer).

Entrepreneurial Spirit

In a widely recognized study conducted for the Population Reference Bureau, Professor Jeanne Biggar traced the shifts in population that the United States has experienced since 1970. She noted that 15 Sunbelt states had accounted for nearly two-thirds of America's population growth. Biggar pointed out, however, that the real meaning of these shifts was not so much the number of people who were moving to the South and West; instead, it was the *quality* of those who migrated that held ominous implications for the older cities. "The North," Professor Biggar noted, "is losing the able youth who might be most likely to provide the creative ideas and enthusiastic leadership needed to tackle the problems associated with deteriorating cities." In other words, those individuals who approach life with what we referred to as the entrepreneurial advantage.

Many older cities are *not* declining because they are losing their economic base; they are losing their economic base because they are losing the individuals who could breathe life into their economies. No city, state, or country can create or sustain prosperity unless it nourishes individuals who remain alert to changing markets, who can discover opportunities, and who can combine resources in new and better ways to meet the needs of others.

> **Look for areas rich in entrepreneurial talent.**

We always must come back to people. Regardless of the total list of an area's economic advantages and disadvantages, in the final analysis an area's prosperity will be determined largely by the drive of its people. Do the people who live in an area, or are moving into the area, display the entrepreneurial spirit?

Summing Up

When I first began to buy properties in my hometown, I knew nothing about the city's economic base. Quite likely, I couldn't have told you what the term "economic base" meant. But now I do know: I have witnessed first-hand booms, busts, and recoveries in Dallas, Texas, San Diego, California, and Vancouver, British Columbia. I know that a strong local economy can help turn real estate investors into multimillionaires. I also know that a downward slide, even when temporary, can turn unprepared investors upside down.

Even if you're a short-term fix and flipper, closely monitor your area's basic sources of jobs, income, and wealth. If the economic signals start flashing yellow, pay attention. Don't think you can blindly speed through without danger.

Just as importantly, use your knowledge of economic base to help you select geographic areas and communities that show the most long-run promise. Discover those cities, suburbs, or even neighborhoods that will experience high rates of growing demand over the next 5, 10, or 15 years. Had I understood the basics of what I have laid out for you in this chapter at the start of my career, I would have chosen to invest somewhere other than Terre Haute. Or, perhaps I would have targeted a more promising part of the Terre Haute urban area than those neighborhoods where I actually did buy. At very least, I would have recognized my properties were unlikely to achieve the same rates of appreciation as those of William Nickerson. Properties across the United States—or even throughout the same metro area—seldom increase in value at a uniform pace. Rather, those properties appreciate fastest where growing demand pushes against a constrained supply.

> **Focus on cities, communities, and neighborhoods with long-run promise.**

So, put this knowledge to work. Before you invest, follow the advice of Harold Hill (the *Music Man*)—"You gotta know the territory."

CHAPTER 4

Size Up the Competition

After you have found one or more geographic areas where the local economic base looks stable, strong, and growing, invest some time and effort into size up the housing competition. Your competitive survey can pay big dividends because the great majority of investors who own small income properties rarely, if ever, conduct any type of organized competitive market analysis.

In fact, most property owners never even solicit market feedback from their own tenants and rental applicants. As a result, they misprice their units, fail to make the best profit-enhancing improvements, eschew innovation, and, in general, operate their properties with sub-par performance. Fortunately for you, this sub-par management spells big profits for real estate entrepreneurs.

The Competitive Battle

Think of it like this. You're a coach, and your team has won a spot in the playoffs. Do you believe that you would increase your chance of winning if you closely studied the previous game films of your competitors? Of course you would. Every winning coach learns all that he can about the competitors that he will battle for

Winning coaches study their competition.

the championship title. This same principle holds true in real estate. Study your competitors; then craft your game strategy to outplay them.

Four Good Reasons to Conduct a Competitive Market Analysis

Stated more precisely, your competitive real estate market analysis can boost your performance in at least four important ways:

1. Select the best area in which to invest.
2. Use the power of market information to successfully negotiate with sellers.
3. Learn the strengths and weaknesses of competitors such that you can wow your tenants with an outstanding value proposition.
4. Develop more accurate property appraisals and financial pro formas.

Where to Invest

Your economic base analysis leads you to those areas of employment strength and population growth. You're looking for people with money, but the other side of demand is supply. When too many investors, developers, and homebuilders all enter the same territory, they sometimes bid up prices to unsustainable heights at the same time they are bringing forth tons of new housing, apartment, and condominium developments. Sooner or later, the market is awash in product. Vacancies shoot up and rent levels fall.

Texas in the Mid 1980s   Texas in the early to mid 1980s serves as Exhibit No. 1 to illustrate this point. Then as now, Texas was a bright star for economic growth, but the Texas real estate developers went wild in speculative overbuilding. Between 1980 and 1985, they threw up hundreds of thousands of apartments and condo projects. Even without the collapse of oil prices, the Texas housing market could not possibly have absorbed all of these new properties at prices and rent levels high enough to turn a profit.

Fortunately, I saw this oversupply coming on stream and liquidated my portfolio of Texas properties one year prior to the peak. Although I would like to claim credit for extraordinarily shrewd market analysis, I fear that boast would substantially overstate the truth of the matter. In that instance, anyone who paid the slightest attention to the public data on housing starts, job growth, and population could have easily forecast a serious downturn in the market.

> **Factor overbuilding into your market strategy.**

Learn from the Texas Experience   Since the disastrous overbuilding of the 1980s, construction lenders have severely tightened their lending practices. In addition, most of the rapid-fire, gun-slinging developers have been killed off. I don't forecast any similar Texas-sized downturns on the horizon.

Nevertheless, overbuilding can still dampen growth markets. As I write, both the Chicago and Atlanta rental markets show signs of softening due to large amounts of recent construction. If I were buying in either of those geographic areas right now, I would pick my neighborhoods and market niches very carefully. I would look for pockets of market opportunity that could withstand the competition that increasing rent concessions are likely to bring.

In addition, I would concentrate on buying only those properties that are bargain -priced and ripe for value-enhancing improvements. When market signals such as rent concessions and rising vacancies flash yellow, it's time to tap the brakes, slow down, and take a more careful look.

Buy When the Blood Is Running in the Streets   Certainly, you want to proceed with caution at the early stages of oversupply. But after vacancy rates, rent levels, and apartment prices ebb, it's time to start buying. By the early 1990s, you could have hung the Homes for Sale classified ad section of the *Dallas Morning News* on the wall; then, to select properties, simply throw darts. In that totally depressed housing market (yet still backed up by strong economic and population growth), nearly any real estate investment strategy would have paid off with outsized returns. Likewise for the San Diego (or even the Inland Empire) housing markets of the mid 1990s.

> **Overbuilding soon turns into shortages.**

Where and when will the blood run next? I can't say for sure right now. You can bet, though, that somewhere at some time, oversupply will again wreak havoc on an otherwise long-term, sound, local economy. And once again, those who are willing to step in and clean up the mess when others see nothing but despair will win big.

Market Information Gives You Negotiating Power and Confidence

When you start shopping to buy your income properties, most sellers give you some sort of rent roll that ostensibly confirms the rents they are collecting for their rental units. Can you believe these owner figures? Maybe, maybe not. Should you faithfully rely on these rent figures to calculate your purchase price and future cash flows? Absolutely not!

To negotiate with power and confidence, you must never, never, never—do I make myself clear?—never rely on the rental income or expense figures that sellers or their real estate agents hand you. You must always work up your own figures based on firsthand knowledge of the rental market. You gain this knowledge only by actually looking at a broad sampling of "for rent" properties, detailing their characteristics and rental rates, and then keeping tabs to see how quickly various types of units rent up.

> **Rely on your own numbers, not the sellers'.**

Sellers' Figures: Too High or Too Low   Sellers routinely overstate their rent collections. To negotiate effectively, you must use your firsthand market data to gently inform the seller that you're not buying his make believe world. Even if the figures were true, a higher than market rent level will probably create more tenant turnover and higher vacancies. For most owners, higher than market rents don't necessarily lead to higher profits.

On some occasions, sellers who lack good market knowledge will charge rents that sit below market. In that case, of course, calculate your bid price according to the seller's figures. You use your knowledge of the market to gain the confidence that you're negotiating a great buy (subject, naturally, to your due diligence property inspections).

"You Can Easily Raise the Rents"   Many sellers will show you their ostensibly below-market rents and then add, "But I deserve a much higher price because after you take over the property you can easily raise the rents." Reject this ploy.

Tell the seller that you're paying for the current operations of the property. You're looking for an investment, not a speculation. "Of course, Mr. Seller, if you're willing to provide me a rent guarantee of those amounts over the next five years, perhaps we could price the property using a higher income stream." Unless you truly do see huge upside potential that extends well beyond the seller's figures, pay only for the present. Reserve the upside as a reward for your entrepreneurial efforts.

> **Pay for the present, not the future.**

Searching for a Preferred Value Proposition (PVP)

After you gain ownership of a rental property, you will improve its operations and market strategy. But how do you know which improvements give you the most profitable competitive edge? By conducting a competitive market analysis (CMA).

As you inspect and evaluate the rental units that are available, take note of every detail that prospective tenants would like or dislike. You're consistently looking for the strengths and weaknesses, advantages and disadvantages of various properties. As you take note of these features, attributes, and turn-ons and turn-offs, you formulate your own strategic action list of dos and don'ts. With your superior knowledge of competing properties, you can positively differentiate your units from those units offered by other investors. Your target market of tenants will quickly see that you're offering the value proposition that they prefer (the PVP).

Constructing Your Financial Pro Formas

You're not buying rental properties merely to wow your tenants with an outstanding product. You want to make money.

Thus, your CMA not only alerts you to the profitable improvements that you can implement, it also steers you clear of those grandiose plans that tenants would not be willing to pay for. If your CMA shows neighborhood rents for two bedroom units typically range between $700 and $850 per month, $850 sets the maximum rent that you're going to be able to collect. Forget the Jacuzzi, the Corian countertops, and the Sub-Zero refrigerator. These improvements won't give you a satisfactory payback.

> **Your CMA leads you to big-profit improvements.**

All too often, I've seen beginning investors (and homeowners) get carried away with their property upgrades only to learn that they've put more money into their improvements than the market (tenants/buyers) will bear. When you temper your plans against the reality of competitive pricing, you strike that profitable balance between too little and too much. Your CMA answers the important question: "If I make these improvements, how much more will tenants be willing and able to pay each month for these units?"

Remember, your target market of tenants live within a budget. When constructing your financial pro formas for future rent collections, capital outlays, and expenses, you must persistently and realistically weigh potential inflows against outflows. You don't want to price your units out of the market. Rather, you want to provide your tenants with the best deal they can get for the amount of money they can afford to spend. You must always work the numbers as you work on the property.

Identify Your Competitors

In a narrow sense, your property will face competition from similarly priced apartment rentals that are located in the same neighborhood. But more broadly (and more realistically), your competition may include rental apartment units in other areas of town as well as houses, co-ops, and condominiums that are offered as rentals. In addition, for many tenant segments, you may face competition from home ownership (single family houses, co-ops, or condominiums). In fact, during the years 2000 to 2003, apartment rent levels and occupancy rates suffered because low interest rates enticed millions of renters into buying their own homes. "Why rent when you can own?" became the competitive battle cry of real estate agents and homebuilders.

> **Your competitors may sit across the street, or across town.**

Quickly Adapt to Change

When you seek to identify your potential competition, answer the question, "What other properties and types of properties might attract the same types of tenants that I'm aiming for?" Then stay abreast of the features and pricing of these alternatives.

If a new 200-unit condo project comes onto the market with "zero-down financing and payments less than rent," you should re-main quick and flexible to fire off a competitive response. Otherwise, your units may begin to incur more turnover, higher vacancies, and ten-ant resistance to rent increases. Never forget that most people shop and compare. They're looking for their best deal wherever they can find it. You must always stand ready to change your strategy as the relative prices of apart-ments, homes, and condos change.

> **Give your tenants the best deal they can find.**

By consistently monitoring the market, you won't get blind-sided when competition heats up—no matter where or what type of property is creating the competitive pressure.

When Markets Tighten

In the short run, competition can make it more difficult for you to generate strong operating profits. Yet, over the long run, you will undoubtedly benefit from the general trend of inflation and in-creasing rents. Over time, as you broadly monitor rent levels, va-cancies, and home prices, your knowledge of the market will help you quickly set your rents at higher levels as demand increases. Apartment owners who don't closely monitor the current market not only tend to overprice themselves out of soft markets, they also fail to adjust their rents upward when the market turns in their favor.

Some property owners I know simply increase their rental rates by 4 or 5 percent every year. In practice, this policy will not maximize profits. In slow markets, their vacancies increase and their tenant quality deteriorates. In tight markets, their rents lag be-hind. In either type of market, the competitive ignorance of these property owners leads to lower performance than they could oth-erwise achieve.

More Practical Implications

During 2000 to 2003, when home prices shot up and rents soft-
ened, prospective tenants asked themselves, "Why pay $1,000 a
month in rent when for that monthly payment
(after our tax deduction) we could buy a
$200,000 house?" But now, with softened rents
and skyrocketing housing prices, many tenants
can no longer afford to buy. Renting looks more
affordable. If (when) mortgage interest rates
start climbing, millions of hopeful first-time
homebuyers will again be forced to continue
renting. Investors who are first to notice this
shift can position themselves to take advantage of it. I believe that
the next three to five years will show much stronger rental markets and concurrently increasing prices for small income properties.

> **High home prices
> will soon force
> more young
> people to rent.**

What to Look For: The Location

When you evaluate and compare competitive properties, first
closely detail the features of their respective locations. Superficially, you might rate the locations as say, excellent, good, okay, or
"let's get out of here quick." But savvy investors go deeper. In fact,
the concept of location actually includes dozens of major and
minor key ingredients that impact tenant appeal. As a minimum,
consider the following:

- ◆ Aesthetics
- ◆ School districts
- ◆ Property taxes and services
- ◆ Crime rates
- ◆ Accessibility
- ◆ Trendiness

◆ Public transportation

◆ Neighborhood residents (existing and newcomers)

In an ideal world, all of your competitive properties would perfectly match each other on every possible mea-
sure of location. Regrettably, such perfection is
seldom found. More than likely you will discover
significant locational differences (both favorable
and unfavorable). When you do, you must adjust
your estimate of tenant appeal either up or
down accordingly. You must carefully isolate
each difference; otherwise you can miss a fea-
ture that can provide a competitive advantage or disadvantage.

> **"Location" refers
> to a wide variety
> of ingredients.**

Aesthetics

To truly understand and identify the features of a neighborhood,
drive the streets very slowly. At times, get out of your car and walk
about. Focus your attention on the neighborhood's overall attractiveness and appeal. Talk with residents. What do they like or dislike? Search for answers to questions such as these:

1. *Noise.* Does the neighborhood suffer from any undue
    traffic noise, airport flight paths, industrial sounds, or
    other disturbances (loud barking dogs, nearby construc-
    tion, and so on)?

2. *Upkeep.* Do owners and tenants maintain their proper-
    ties? Do homes and apartment buildings sparkle with
    pride of ownership, or do many properties need paint
    and yard maintenance?

3. *Parking.* Are the streets relatively free of cars, or does
    the neighborhood lack sufficient off-street driveways and
    garages? Worse yet, do you see cars parked in yards?
    (Neighborhoods heavy with student rentals sometimes
    display this type of eyesore.)

4. ***Bad mix.*** Does the neighborhood abut or merge into any commercial, industrial, or otherwise incompatible land uses? Do you notice unsightly vacant lots and run-down or boarded-up properties?

5. ***Views.*** Do neighborhood residents enjoy pleasant views of lakes, parks, woods, bays, or mountains?

6. ***Overall feel.*** What's your overall feel of the neighborhood? Does it seem to be moving up, stable, or moving down?

School Districts

If tenant households include school-age children, school district quality can boost or retard rental rates. Don't overlook this feature. Unlike your own home, though, you need not buy your investment property in the best—or even a good—school district. It all depends on their relative prices, rent levels, and the types of tenants you hope to attract to your property.

I have frequently found that it's wise to avoid properties in top school districts because investors and homebuyers bid purchase prices up too high. I am quite willing to sacrifice an unknown amount of future appreciation in favor of more cash flow in my pocket today. Work the numbers in your area for yourself. What is true in one city or neighborhood might not stand true elsewhere. Nevertheless, don't mistakenly overlook the less prestigious school districts. In many cities, fewer than 20 percent of rental households include school-age children.

> **Less prestigious school districts often make good investments.**

Property Taxes and Services

In too many towns and cities, high property taxes can eat into rent receipts. Before you avoid high taxes per se, though, compare government services. High property taxes undermine values only when area residents don't receive a commensurate high level of government benefits. In addition to schools, government services may provide parks, recreation areas, golf courses, community colleges, trash collection, water, and sewers, as well as police, fire, and other protective services.

Should you find that two competitive properties are subject to different amounts of property taxes, look further. You may also

> **Find out what government services you get for the taxes you will pay.**

find that they differ in their level of municipal and county services. In some instances, you may even discover that lower-rate taxing districts offer a higher level of services. In any event, realize that tenants of some buildings will enjoy a level of government services that aren't available to the tenants in other areas. Rental rates can reflect this difference.

Crime Rates

Naturally, people want to feel safe in their apartments and on their neighborhood streets. Low crime makes for higher property values and monthly rents, but it's not just the quantity of crime that counts. More important is the type of crime. Drug dealing, gang shootouts, and house break-ins weigh much differently than occasional car thefts or those domestic squabbles that bring in the police.

Quite often, too, perceptions of neighborhood crime don't match reality. Check facts with the police. Also, recognize that statistical reporting areas may not accurately apply to various submarket neighborhoods. Beware of broad-sweeping generalizations. Pinpoint as closely as possible the actual street boundaries that delineate high-crime areas. Sometimes you can locate pockets of relative safety. As good people flee to this oasis, rents and property values will go up.

Accessibility

How quickly and surely can you travel from a neighborhood to job centers, shopping, professional services, recreation areas, schools, colleges, and cultural facilities? Are streets often congested? Does most to-and-from traffic flow through a nightmare-type interchange (such as Atlanta's famous spaghetti junction, perhaps more aptly named malfunction junction)? Do frequent auto accidents leave traffic stalled? What about tolls? They can mount up. Is the neighborhood served by just one bridge, or numerous ways in and out? Tenants typically value convenient accessibility even more than most homeowners (who for the most part migrate to suburbia).

Trendiness

For some tenant segments, trendiness has become a much sought-after feature. How does the neighborhood rate for coffee houses, ethnic restaurants, bookstores, and movie theaters (especially those that show foreign and independent films)? That advertising come-on, "Walk to chic shops, restaurants, and cafes," will bring a nice rent premium for properties that offer this desirable convenience. If the neighborhood lacks these in-places now, do any signs show their arrival? Has Starbuck's shown interest in the area?

Public Transportation

In some cities, apartment buildings within convenient walking distance of a commuter train (or subway) station rent for as much as 5 to 10 percent more than quite comparable units located slightly farther away. Rental units near bus stops don't typically command the price premium they used to but for some tenants, this feature still proves to be an advantage worth paying for. As for other types of public transportation (taxis, airports, ferries, limousine service), easy availability may or may not affect a property's rent levels. You must learn the tenant and homebuyer market to tell for sure.

Who Are the Residents and Recent Homebuyers and Tenants?

Whenever you compare locations (neighborhoods), learn who lives there now and who's moving in. What are their professions, educations, ages, incomes, lifestyles, races, religions, and family sizes? Though it's true that fair housing laws bar discrimination, it's obvious that few neighborhoods in the United States perfectly mirror demographic diversity. Today we find considerable voluntary congregation of Blacks, Latinos, Jews, Asians, seniors, young urban professionals, and various other demographic mixes.

> **Who's moving in? Who's moving out?**

Today, many neighborhood racial and ethnic changes push values up—not down, as many stereotypical beliefs hold. For our brief purposes here, though, note that people influence rent levels and property values. And although fair housing laws forbid real estate agents and property managers from taking notice of the racial, ethnic, and religious characteristics of neighborhoods, investors need not avert their eyes and ignore reality.

Apart from demographics, notice whether neighborhood properties are primarily occupied by owners or renters. Similar to race, ethnicity, religion, and other personal characteristics, you can't judge owners or renters as always better or worse, per se. Instead, you must weigh and consider. What are the implications for a property's rental rates? On occasion, in neighborhoods experiencing gentrification, for example, you may find younger, upscale renters displacing moderate-income homeowners. Nevertheless, when possible, I prefer to buy multi-unit buildings in predominantly single-family neighborhoods—if I can buy them at a reasonable price. Likewise, condo units in buildings with higher owner occupancy tend to rent for a higher price than condo buildings that are flooded with renters.

Site Features

After you've detailed how competing properties compare in terms of location, you can next turn to the site features of specific properties. You would especially note such potentially appealing features such as landscaping, yard care, spacious grounds, on-site parking, fencing, and amenities such as swimming pool, tennis courts, clubhouse, or fitness center.

In viewing the site and site amenities, try to identify those attractive features that stand in short supply; then, when you enter the market to buy, you'll be able to quickly recognize those features that place a property at a competitive advantage or disadvantage. Of course, this same principle holds true for the exterior and interior of properties.

The Exterior of the Building

As you inspect the exteriors of various competitive properties, note their aesthetics, state of repair, construction materials such as brick, block, or frame, number of stories, and architectural style.

Do the buildings seem modern and functional or outdated? Notice points of access to the units. Can tenants park reasonably

> **Do competitors maintain their properties?**

close to the building or rental unit entry points? How much curb appeal do the buildings and grounds typically show? Does the property condition invite potential tenants to come in and take a look? Or would it encourage apartment seekers to drive up, take one glance, and immediately drive right off, thus abandoning their appointment to view a vacant unit.

Would the property itself raise any security issues with potential tenants? Are first-floor windows protected by security screens or other preventive measures? Are the parking areas, walkways, and building entrances well lighted?

Remember—you want to view these competing properties through the eyes of potential tenants. Far too many investors overlook the actual appeal and livability of properties. Instead, they unduly focus on rents and expenses. While rents and expenses do determine the bottom line, it is the appeal of the property from the tenant's perspective that in the end accounts for the figures that work themselves down to that bottom line.

"Play the Tenant"

Before you invest in a rental property, I strongly encourage you to "play the tenant." By "play the tenant," I mean go through the basic search process just as would a real tenant. Read the rental ads. Call to make further inquiry. Go out and look at the actual houses and apartments that are currently available for rent. Learn about the various tenant application procedures, leases, and damage deposits that owners and managers use. Also, evaluate the total marketing effort including the quality of the advertising, the professionalism of the showing, and any follow-up activities.

With this information in hand, you can learn to differentiate among those property owners (managers) who get their properties rented, and those whose units remain on the market for an extended amount of time. By actually looking at units and talking with rental agents, you will gain a wealth of knowledge that you can then turn into real wealth.

Inspecting the Interiors of Competing Rental Units

With pleasing grounds and a good building exterior, investors can typically draw tenants in to look at their available rental units; however, without a pleasing interior, most good tenants will continue their search. What are those features that contribute to a pleasing interior? Probably many of those same features that attracted you to your current home.

- ◆ Aesthetics
- ◆ Livability: unit size, room count, and floor plan
- ◆ Utility bills

Aesthetics: How Does the Unit Look, Feel, and Sound?

"I was once in a home," recalls real estate appraiser Dodge Woodson, "that made me feel as if there should have been a coffin sitting in the living room. The drapes were dark and heavy—a ghastly green that gave me an eerie feeling. I don't spook easily, and I'm used to seeing a lot of homes in a lot of different conditions, but this home made me uncomfortable. If I had been a prospective buyer or tenant, I would not have been able to focus on anything but the drapes."

Woodson's reaction to this house with the eerie dark green drapes wouldn't have surprised Professor Mary Jasmosli of George Washington University. Jasmosli has developed an expertise she calls environmental sensitivity. Through her research she has found that people react emotionally to interior living areas in ways that they themselves can neither explain nor understand. "Home features such as number of windows, window treatments, color schemes, views, placement of walls and doorways, room size, ceiling height, cleanliness, and the amount of light all hold special meaning," reports Jasmosli.

> **Rental units should display emotional appeal.**

Now, we'll return to Dodge Woodson. "The next time I entered that home, I couldn't believe the difference," he remarks. "The owners had replaced the dark green drapes with flowing white window treatments. . . . Not only was the living area pretty, it appeared much larger. . . . I noticed features that I had never seen before. The rooms were alive with light. This experience convinced me of the power that window treatments have."

To the extent your aesthetic sensibilities permit, critique the emotional impact of the living areas that you inspect. Pay close attention to everything from window treatments to ceiling heights, from color schemes to the placement of walls and doorways. Will potential tenants react as Dodge Woodson did on his first visit to the home he describes, or will they respond more as he did on his second visit?

Livability: Unit Size, Room Count, and Floor Plan

After you have moved beyond the aesthetics of a rental unit, next evaluate its floor plan. Does the layout of the living area offer convenience and privacy, and does it work efficiently?

When you first approach the main entry, do you have to climb steep steps? Is there a covered area so visitors can avoid standing in the rain or snow while waiting for someone inside to answer their knock? If the main entrance lies below grade, does it appear that water may build up in the entrance area? As you walk in the front door, notice whether you're dropped immediately into a living area or if the unit has a foyer. Is there an adequate-sized coat closet nearby? Relative to the main entrance, where is the kitchen located? Can you walk from the entry door to other rooms of the unit without passing through a third room? How are the locations and sizes of bedrooms, baths, and closets?

> **Livability generates higher rents and lower turnover.**

Now imagine tenants living in the apartment. Where will their kids play, both indoors and outdoors? Will the parents be able to keep an eye on them? If you're looking at a larger-sized unit, does it have a "Grand Central Station" living room, or is this room pleasantly isolated from other activity areas?

Go into the kitchen. How long does it take the faucet to draw hot water? For purposes of work efficiency, can someone step conveniently between the refrigerator, oven, stovetop, and sink? Do you see adequate counter and cabinet space? How much natural and artificial light is there? Is there an eat-in kitchen area that separates the household members who are eating from those who are working (preparing meals, cleaning up)? Is there easy access to the kitchen from an outside entrance of the unit's main entrance? Can someone conveniently enter the kitchen from the parking area while carrying several bags of groceries?

Noise is a potential problem within many rental units. Does sound from a television or stereo carry into other rooms? You might even bring along a portable radio on your inspections. Place it in various rooms. Turn the volume up. Do the walls provide enough soundproofing? Roommate-type tenants want privacy and quiet. If a property fails to offer these essentials, it will lose tenants and rents.

Just as important, will tenants be able to hear neighbors or neighborhood noise from inside the unit? Again, tenants pay for quiet. They discount heavily for noise.

Although potential neighbors and neighborhood noise are especially important to notice in neighborhoods filled with apartment buildings, predominantly single-family neighborhoods are no strangers to loud stereos, barking dogs, and Indy 500 engine revving. Don't just assume that the neighborhood offers peace and quiet to a building's tenants. Verify peace and quiet with the property's owner, manager, or current residents.

Utility Bills

When you're viewing competitive units, inquire about utility bills in two ways. Who pays what? How energy efficient is the unit?

Who Pays What?   Although relatively few property owners today run "all bills paid" types of rental buildings, many owners do pay water, sewage, cable, heat, trash collection, or some combination thereof. To compare rental units and their respective rent levels fairly, you need to know which if any utility bills are included in the monthly rent figure. In colder climates, for example, a rent of $1,000 per month that covers heating costs could actually prove to be a lower cost than another unit that rented for $950 a month—no bills paid.

How Energy Efficient Are the Units?   Energy efficiency affects the rentability of rental units in two ways. One way is comfort. Units that lack good insulation tend to dissipate heat or air conditioning much too quickly, causing uncomfortable changes in temperatures, cold air, drafts, and possibly hot spots. The other way is cost. As we all know, poor insulation and energy-guzzling HVAC and appliances send utility bills through the roof.

> **Tenants flee rental units with high-cost utilities.**

Either or both of these conditions will increase a building's tenant turnover, vacancies, and rent levels. Today, smart tenants verify energy efficiency before they sign a lease. It's perfectly reasonable for you to seek answers about energy efficiency, examine the HVAC and hot water units, and check the windows and exterior doors for drafts. You could also ask current tenants about their comfort level and the size of their heat, hot water, and cooling bills.

The Rental Process

When tenants shop for a place to live, they primarily consider location, the exterior and interior of the physical property, and the monthly costs (rent, parking fees, utility bills). However, to an extent greater than most property owners realize, tenant choices are also influenced by the total rental process. This process typically starts with the advertising of the units and extends through the ap-

Application and leasing procedures influence tenant choices.

plication procedures, the amount of the required security deposit, the specific terms of the rental agreement, and even the personality and professionalism (or lack thereof) of the person who answers telephone calls from prospective tenants and shows the available units.

As you size up potential competitors, you enhance your ability to craft a winning market strategy when you carefully evaluate the total rental process that most property owners and managers typically follow. Try to discover the advantages that will give your properties a competitive edge—everywhere you can find them.

When very few owners permit pets, maybe you should allow them. When nearly all owners require a 12-month lease, maybe you could profit by permitting shorter terms. When most owners advertise with vague, basic information, perhaps you can gain tenant interest for your units with a more appealing sales message.

We discuss the rental process in a later chapter. For now, recognize that this process does affect the relative appeal and desirability of competing rental units. As you survey rental properties, add these types of data to your storehouse of knowledge.

CHAPTER 5

Go After a Target Market

Let's review where we've been so far and where we're going. Overall, you want to study the economic base of an area, conduct a competitive market analysis, and craft a market strategy that will give your properties a competitive advantage over other property owners. You want to provide a preferred value proposition (PVP) to a select type of tenant. When such tenants look at one of your units, you want them to shout, "Wow! We'll take it. We'll pay whatever you're asking!"

Okay, I'm dreaming. But you get the general idea.

How to Create a PVP

How can you achieve this goal of PVP and still earn a healthy profit? Let's retrace these six steps:

1. Survey the overall strength of the pertinent market area(s) for population growth, jobs, income, wealth, quality of life, number of residential listings for sale and for rent, market values, apartment rent levels, vacancy rates, and other market signals.

2.   Discover all that you can about the competing houses, apartments, and condos that currently attract (or might attract) the type of persons who might make up your target market.

3.   After this overall market survey leads you to one or more promising geographic areas, select a target market of renters. Learn all that you can about these potential renters (the prime topic of this chapter).

4.   Buy a property that you think *could* stand superior to these competitors.

5.   Plan, design, and execute an improvement program for this property.

6.   Develop a total value proposition and a low-cost, highly effective campaign to sell, trade, or lease the property.

What does nearly every business in the country want? Less competition! What kind of markets do most property owners face? Highly competitive! Even relatively small towns and cities typically offer homebuyers and renters hundreds, if not thousands, of choices. How can you consistently earn extraordinary profits in a marketplace filled with tenant choices? Cater to a distinct market with uniquely desirable property features.

> **Establish a competitive advantage through target marketing.**

When you choose a target market and craft your strategy accordingly, tenant demand for your properties will significantly exceed those generic competing properties. For, in fact, those competing properties won't seem comparable at all to the market segment of tenants whom you have chosen to offer a preferred value proposition.

Diversity Rules

The term *diversity* embraces not only gender, race, and religious beliefs. It also includes a complete panorama of demographics and psychographics (emotional feelings, preferences, and attitudes). By contemplating how people differ across a wide range of characteristics, you can zero in on a select bull's eye of tenant customers.

Demographic Differences

Think about the following list of demographic characteristics. Can you see how a property owner might use one or more of these attributes to help segment a market? With these attributes in mind, craft a strategy to meet a motivating need, want, or problem of these people.

- Age
- Years of schooling
- Sex
- Occupation/employer
- Height
- Weight
- Health/disability
- Geographic location
- Household size
- Household composition
- Income/credit score
- Wealth/cash savings
- Stage of life
- Religion
- Ethnicity
- Credit score
- Homeowner/renter
- Marital status

Here are several examples from my experience:

Share-A-Home (Age and Health) Among my properties, I formerly owned a large 3,200 square foot, five-bedroom, four-bath single-family house that I rented out for $850 a month to a married couple with children. But in talking with another rental property owner in the neighborhood, I discovered a much more profitable use for that house.

It turned out that this investor owned four properties in the area and rented rooms in each of these large houses to individual seniors. Typically, these people were age 70 or older. They were healthy enough to care for their own basic everyday living, but not up to maintaining their own private residence. The investor essentially operated these properties as high-class boarding houses. He called these houses Share-A-Homes.

Subsequently, I learned that blind luck had favored me. Not only was my house located within a Share-A-Home zoning district, but also, with no changes whatsoever, it met the strict regulatory housing codes that applied to this type of rental property (that is, size of bedrooms, number of bathrooms, number and location of exits, window locks, kitchen facilities, and so on). Although I had no interest in personally running a Share-A-Home, I did lease the house to the operator down the street. My new rent: $1,350 per month.

> **Increase rents with target marketing.**

Share-A-Homes Update: Tropical Village, Inc.   Just a couple of weeks ago, I responded to a real estate ad (see Exhibit 5.1) in the Wednesday property edition of the *Wall Street Journal*. The ad headline promised investors a 30 percent cash-on-cash return. When I received the promotional packet, I was amazed to see that the development company soliciting investor funds, Tropical Village, Inc., was building new, upscale Share-A-Homes in a triplex format. Here's an excerpt from the enclosed promotional letter (for the full letter, see Exhibit 5.2):

> There is no other product in the rental market within our rent range that offers the amenities [fitness center, heated swimming pool, beauty salon, card and super bowl room, putting green, shuffleboard, maid service] that we are offering. Our target market for rental is the senior that cannot quite handle the daily upkeep of a home or apartment, yet they are healthy and are not ready for the assisted living type of care. . . . Seniors can keep their independence longer.

Tropical Village is aiming to provide their target markets of investors and residents a value proposition that's tough to beat.

30 % RETURN*

NEW 3 Story Triplexes

For Healthy Seniors
Elevators & Health Club
$670,000 10% Dn. ($67,000)

Includes: Mgmt & Financing

1031's OK/Recession Proof

Toll Free: (877) 542-6251

***Projected Rate of Return**

Exhibit 5.1 Ad for Tropical Village Triplex.

Given the sellout and rent-up rates of their previous Share-A-Home developments, they seem to be succeeding.

Other Possibilities You can slice and dice demographics in thousands of different combinations. Because you're renting one building at a time, you could pinpoint the needs of a quite narrow type of person, family, or household. One renovator I knew specifically tailored his various rental properties to better accommodate roommate living, families with young children, or families with teenage children. Wheelchair-friendly units also seem to be in short supply relative to demand. Some property owners target the

Tropical Village, Inc.

GRAN PARK AT SOUTHPARK • 8517 SOUTH PARK CIRCLE • SUITE 210 • ORLANDO, FL 32819
(407) 354-0004 • FAX (407) 354-1112 • TOLL FREE (877) 542-6251

August 30, 2002

Dear Dr. Eldred:

Thank you for your interest in Pelican Bay Club.

I am sure that you are aware of the growing number of senior citizens within the State of Florida. Florida is second only to California in senior population and growth and it is a proven fact that seniors are living longer and staying physically healthier.

As a developer of senior housing we have found that there is a great need within the State for affordable senior housing. The information that we have received from the different senior councils and the housing authorities has reinforced our market studies.

We at Tropical Village, Inc. have developed a unique style of rental housing that services the needs of today's seniors. Our goal is to build safe and affordable housing for the healthy, active senior. The two major concerns of seniors and their families are safety and lack of family or social contact. Many seniors have a major problem with loneliness and the lack of interaction with other people. When this happens the seniors have a tendency to fail physically and mentally.

I would like to explain the type of housing that we build. Our developments consist of individual three-story triplexes. Each floor has five bedrooms with individual bathrooms, a shared kitchen and a shared living room. Think of student housing only specialized for today's seniors. These triplexes are fully furnished and the kitchens are fully equipped. Each floor has a laundry room, computer room with a computer and printer and high-speed internet service. In addition to being fully furnished, the bedrooms have a wall safe, ceiling fan, and are key locked for privacy. The living room has a 25″ color TV with a VCR. We also offer the Guardian Medical Alert for those who may request that. Our seniors have a homey atmosphere that is very upscale.

We have been advised that seniors, especially single seniors, like this shared living concept; they actually like having the interaction with other seniors and generally form little family-type groups. We try to make each floor coed, and with the help of the local

Figure 5.2   Example of Target Marketing.

senior organizations and social groups, we are able to have a program of activities in place for our healthy seniors. We have a doctors group that will make house calls, a pharmacy company that delivers prescriptions and gives lectures, home health care and physical therapy on site.

The Osceola Council on Aging held 15 focus group studies on our shared living product with over 200 participants, and the approval rate was over 75 percent. The focus groups were from very diversified groups of seniors.

The triplexes are joined together by high-speed elevators. The senior developments will have many amenities such as a fitness center, heated swimming pool, beauty salon, card and super bowl room, minibus, putting green, shuffleboard, and professional management on site. After an extensive interview process both in Florida and Atlanta we have chosen Premier Management Group to manage our project in Kissimmee, Florida, Atlanta, Georgia, Pasco County, Florida and they will also manage our newest development, Pelican Bay Club in Palm Bay, Florida. I have enclosed their resume for your review. The triplexes are furnished by a design group called C.V.C. with ceramic tile and Berber carpet.

There is no other product in the rental market within our rent range that offers the amenities that we are offering. Our target market for rental is the senior that cannot quite handle the daily upkeep of a home or apartment, yet they are healthy and are not ready for the assisted living hospital type of care. With the on-site services that we bring onto the development, seniors can stay longer and keep their independence longer.

Each triplex is rented by the bedroom at the rate of **$675.00 per month for nine bedrooms and $775.00 per month for six bedrooms. Each triplex generates rent on fifteen bedrooms. This rent includes all utilities, phone, satellite cable, and maid service twice per week** (in the kitchen, living room and laundry room), plus all of the amenities on the site. The bedrooms are all pre-wired for satellite cable and telephone service. Our communities are **gated** for the safety of the seniors.

Our project, Harbor Bay in Kissimmee, Florida, is completely sold out and the first tenants are moving in. Our management team is in the process of leasing these units. We were part of two large senior expos within the last few months and we are happy to say they were very successful. Summerhill in Atlanta, Georgia, is sold out, the land has been purchased, and we hope to start construction in approximately six to eight weeks once the construction financing is firmly in place.

Our project in Port Richey, Florida, Sunset Bay Club, has completely sold out of both Phase I and Phase II. Our construction is in process and we will start pre-leasing in October of this year.

(continued)

Figure 5.2   *(Continued)*

We are now in the process of pre-selling Pelican Bay Club in Palm Bay which is located in Brevard County on the east coast of Florida. We chose this location due to the high amount of senior citizens.

As I mentioned above, **each triplex has fifteen bedrooms, nine bedrooms rent for $675.00 per month and six larger bedrooms rent for $775.00 per month.** The cost of the triplex is $690,000. The way to purchase this investment is as follows: We require a deposit of 10 percent which is paid as follows: $6,000 is to be submitted with the contract, and goes into the development of the project. If you cannot for any reason get your funding, this money is refundable. The balance of $63,000 will be required to be sent to the title company at the time Tropical Village, Inc. is ready to purchase the land and go to construction. Tropical Village, Inc. will pay up to 3 percent of the loan amount in closing costs for you. This will be approximately $18,600.00. We pay this to offset the time that you will be waiting for your triplex to be built.

The net cash flow after all expenses and mortgage payment is approximately $28,000 annually. Enclosed please find a cash flow figure sheet and some general information.

The Evans Group, and Parsons Architectural Co. designed our units and we are very proud of the quality of living that our seniors will experience within all of our projects. Winter Park Construction has been our builder for our last two projects and we have complete confidence in their ability to build excellent projects.

Please call me when you receive this packet so that we can go over it together. My toll free number is **(877) 542–6251. I would also like to extend an invitation to you to come to my Orlando office and I would be glad to show you the site and also go over the building plans.**

Per our conversation we deal with three lenders. The name of one is CTX Mortgage Company the phone # is 561-471-0213 and the contact's name is Lynn Stevens. I will have the other names and numbers available when we speak again.

Sincerely,

Linda S. Beaver
Sales Manager

Figure 5.2   *(Continued)*

> **Different people mean different wants, different needs.**

financially responsible, yet cash- or credit-impaired renter. One of my previous properties was located two blocks from a hospital. I fixed up the property and drafted a rental agreement that when brought together made these units especially appealing to younger, single nurses.

Psychographic Differences

> **Lifestyle marketing focuses on specific attitudes and values.**

Most property owners (especially the larger developers, homebuilders, and apartment complexes) combine demographics with psychographics to create their target markets. In this sense, I'm using the term *psychographics* to refer to all types of mental predispositions such as likes, dislikes, tastes, preferences, attitudes, values, and lifestyle. Again quoting from the Tropical Village promotional letter (Exhibit 5.2):

Our goal is to offer safe and affordable housing to the healthy, active senior. Many seniors have a major problem with loneliness and lack of interaction with other people. . . . [Therefore] seniors like this shared-living concept . . . and generally form little family-type groups. . . . We are able to sponsor a program of activities for our residents.

Here you can see how Tropical Village blends demographic characteristics such as old age and reasonably good health with psychographic characteristics such as active lifestyle, social interaction, and safety. Most importantly, you can see how the firm is trying to understand the needs and wants of their target audience, and craft their apartment units, amenities, and services to meet those needs.

Myrtle Beach Condominiums   Some years back, I was called in as a marketing research consultant by a developer in Myrtle Beach, SC, who was trying to get financing to build a condominium project. Unfortunately for this developer, his lender thought he was nuts. Why? Because at that time, the national economy was mired in a deep recession, gasoline prices were shooting up, and, of no small concern, the local Myrtle Beach housing market was littered with unsold see-through, mid-rise, beachfront condo projects.[1]

But this developer wasn't crazy. He had studied his target market segment very well. He knew that as one of the premier golfing centers in the United States, Myrtle Beach attracted hundreds of thousands of visitors each year who cared nothing about the Atlantic Ocean and Grand Strand beaches. These visitors come to play golf all day; and eat seafood, drink, and share camaraderie with friends all evening. These golfing buddies didn't need or want an expensive, beachfront condo (or hotel). They wanted comfortable, private, and spacious accommodations at an economy price.

The developer's value proposition: A 1,350 square foot townhouse-style, two-bedroom, two-bath condo, situated 14 blocks west of the beach, yet within 15 minutes of most popular golf courses. Because of this "off-the-beaten-path" location, the developer was able to price the units 60 percent less than the condo price levels that created the beachfront bust. Yet, that wasn't the end of the story.

> **Even "oversupply" doesn't foreclose opportunity.**

The developer knew that many golfing buddies circulate within a group of 6 to 10 (or more) friends. To make the condo units more appealing and affordable, he persuaded potential buyers to split the costs of ownership among perhaps 4, 6, or even 10 partners. When marketed in this way, the golfing buddies were able to obtain housing for either weekend that surpassed the quality of anything comparable in the

---

1. A see-through building is a partially built, abandoned project. Because only the skeleton (frame) of the building has been put up, you can see right through it.

market. And when figured on a per-person, nightly-use basis, at far less cost than the Holiday Inn.

Within 18 months, the developer had sold out the first two phases of the project and was already into planning phase three. In this case, savvy target marketing and product development created huge profits for this astute entrepreneur—even when most other builders were clinging tightly to their worry beads.

Avoid Standard Labels, Picture Your Actual Renters

You may have heard people refer to housing segments as empty-nesters, swinging singles, first-time homebuyers, move-up buyers, the age 55+ market, and more recently, the Hispanic market, the Asian market, and even the Islamic market. SRI (formerly known as the Stanford Research Institute, a Menlo Park firm with whom I've done a little work) developed a market segment classification system known as VALS (an acronym for values and lifestyles) that was unthinkingly used by many new apartment complexes and homebuilders. Included among these VALS segments are such supposed groups as:

- ◆ Survivors
- ◆ Sustainers
- ◆ Achievers

- ◆ Belongers
- ◆ Emulators
- ◆ Societally conscious

Although any or all of the aforementioned labels might stimulate your thinking, never rely on labels to steer your market segmentation strategy. One book for real estate investors, for example, tells its readers to sell their renovated properties to first-time homebuyers. But that label (as do all generic segmentation labels) lacks clarity and precision. I learned that fact in person during the mid to late 1990s when I was offering my Stop Renting Now!™ seminars throughout the country. Quite surprising to me, my seminar attendees fit no specific

> **Avoid broad brush labels.**

demographic. They included a wide range of ages, income, wealth, and family size:

- ◆ Age (25 to 55)
- ◆ Income ($20,000 to $120,000)
- ◆ Cash down available (0–$100,000)
- ◆ Credit score (350–800)
- ◆ Family status (single, divorced, separated, married, married with children, unmarried partners)
- ◆ Race (all races)
- ◆ Lifestyles (all of the values, attitudes, and life situations that anyone could imagine)

However, all of these people did hold one motivating preference in common. They wanted to stop renting and start owning. When you create a target market for your properties, think precisely. Picture clearly in every relevant detail the characteristics (demographics, psychographics, lifestyles, preferences, turn-ons, and turn-offs) of the people whom you would like to impress with your PVP. Then fashion the features of your property and leasing program to appeal to those strong motivations.

College Students   I've heard many owners of rental houses and apartments declare that they avoid renting to "college students." But similar to first-time homebuyers, college students come in all types. My partners and I once renovated a 16-unit apartment building specifically for a target market of college students. That building proved quite profitable, and the students appreciated the way we ran the property to serve their needs and wants.

But we didn't just rent to "college students." We targeted top students, nonsmokers, above-average financial resources, mature in demeanor, quiet, and clean. In return, we offered the students one of the most pleasant places to live at a fair rent level. We achieved our extraordinary profits through lower costs for repairs, advertising, marketing, and management, as well as virtually zero vacancies and bad debts.

Hitting the Bull's Eye

You might begin your thoughts about target marketing with broad brush labels such as sustainers, achievers, college students, first-time buyers, active seniors, empty nesters, young-marrieds, singles, roommates, moderate-income, Section 8s, or even that once ubiquitous segment known as yuppies. Or how about another broad brush segment, burpies (black urban professionals)? And of course, the most popular broad-brush demographic label of all, baby boomers, now followed by Gen Xers, Gen Ys, and echo boomers.

Any of these broad-brush labels might point you toward market segments that share some similar characteristics, but the people within each of these sweeping categories also show critical differences. To hit that most profitable bull's eye within your target market, search for the unique and intense needs that motivate specific people.

Find Unique and Intense Needs

To create a highly profitable value proposition (PVP), find those intense (motivating) needs and wants that other rental property owners are missing. Search for those differences that will make *the* difference for the bull's eye segment of tenants that you plan to serve. For example, I found that the nurses I rented to were especially concerned about safety and security; therefore, I increased the amount of outdoor lighting at the property, installed double dead-bolt door locks, and bolted heavy-gauge wire mesh screens on all of the building's first story windows.

> **Identify your tenants' hot buttons.**

In addition, these nurses wanted far more closet space than the other older rental units in the neighborhood typically provided. Fortunately, the bedrooms in my older building measured at least $14' \times 16'$. That feature allowed me to slice off $2'$ of floor space and add a wall-length closet in each bedroom. As a special touch, I installed full-length mirrors on the new closet doors. This not only played to vanity but also continued the spacious appearance of the bedrooms.

Bull's Eye Lease Assessment

In taking a cue from Doreen Bierbrier (*Managing Your Rental Property for More Income*, McGraw-Hill, 1985), I rented to the nurses individually, rather than as a pre-formed group. I also permitted any nurse to get out of her lease at any time if she would find a substitute tenant that proved acceptable to me and the existing residents of the building. These (primarily younger) women appreciated that flexibility—although few of them exercised this option. In fact, the overall stability of tenants within the property actually surprised me.

Throw Away Standard Operating Procedures

Most owners of small rental properties operate their buildings according to some combination of "standard operating procedure,"

> **Know your customer.**

the detailed directions offered by authors of their favorite real estate books, or the owner's personal insights and idiosyncratic prejudices unguided by a customer (tenant) profile. I urge you to practice a more profitable approach. Before you begin your property search, get to know your intended customer. My experiences and the experiences of other entrepreneurs prove that the more closely you identify and attend to the motivating needs of your potential tenants, the more they will reward you with a higher and more dependable stream of rental income.

In stark contrast to target marketing, those owners who merely offer a generic rental property to a generic tenant earn generic returns at best. If you follow in their path, you will condemn yourself to so-called market rent levels, for that's what "market" refers to: the average rent for a standard, look-alike product in an open and competitive marketplace. No profit-maximizing entrepreneur is willing to compete with a plain Jane generic product.

How Do You Identify the Wow (PVP) Features for Your Tenants?

Because you probably can't read minds, you need some techniques to discover those elements of your value proposition that will motivate your bull's eye tenants to act now. Here are several ideas that have worked for me and other successful rental property owners that I know:

- ◆ Talk informally with people; discover their problems
- ◆ Pay attention, eavesdrop, read, watch.
- ◆ Talk with insiders and experts.
- ◆ Use questionnaires.
- ◆ Conduct (informal) focus groups.

Informal Conversations

Perhaps I'm a born inquisitor. No matter where I am, I like to strike up conversations with people to learn their thoughts, problems, likes, and dislikes. In fact, I discovered the housing opportunity for nurses while visiting one of my parents in the hospital. In casual conversation, I asked a nurse where she lived. That opened the door to one of those "Don't get me started on that" comments.

> **Tenants know what they want. So, ask them.**

That backhanded invitation intensified my inquiry and led to further conversation with the nurse. She then went on to describe how much difficulty she and her workmates encountered when looking for a decent and affordable place to live near the hospital—which is where they preferred to live given their odd-hour work schedules.

Similarly, because I've spent much of my career teaching at universities, I've often relied on informal conversations with students to learn about their housing problems, preferences, likes, and dislikes. These conversations helped me develop my strategy for the 16-unit income property I mentioned earlier in this chapter, as well as other student rentals that I have owned.

How many people do you know (or know of) who have shopped to buy or rent housing in the past year or two. Talk with them. Learn their reactions to the properties they looked at. Why did they eventually choose their current home? What was the difference that made *the* difference for these people? What features would they have liked, yet found rare or unavailable? Talk with people. Ask questions. You'll surprise yourself at how much valuable information you can pick up.

Pay Attention

Read the neighborhood and communities section of your local newspaper. Especially follow those human interest stories as well as Question and Answer columns where people talk about their house hunting and rental problems. When possible, go to your local library and read the articles in the Sunday Real Estate or Homes sections of the *Los Angeles Times,* the *San Diego Union-Tribune,* the *San Francisco Examiner,* the *Chicago Tribune,* or the *Orlando Sentinel,* or the Saturday edition of the *Washington Post.* These newspapers not only feature stories on the latest real estate trends, but most also carry the excellent nationally syndicated columnists, Robert Bruss, Kenneth Harney, and Lew Siechelman.

You can also find good idea-provoking articles in magazines such as *American Demographics,* the *Journal of Property Management,* and *Real Estate Today.* Also, eavesdrop. Perk your ears up when you hear people talking about real estate. Visit several of the many real estate chat rooms on the Internet. Whenever you discover something new or interesting, mull it over. Ask yourself if this fact, trend, or problem could help you better tailor a rental property toward a bull's eye segment of renters. Is there some feature or benefit that you could offer that will strengthen your competitive advantage?

Talk with Insiders and Experts

Every community includes a dozen or more occupations and professions where those employed gain firsthand, insider information by talking directly with homebuyers and renters. To learn more about your market, talk with any of these people:

- ◆ Real estate agents
- ◆ Property managers
- ◆ Bankers
- ◆ Property inspectors
- ◆ Credit counselors
- ◆ Remodeling contractors
- ◆ Real estate investors
- ◆ Newspaper reporters who cover housing and real estate
- ◆ Existing tenants
- ◆ Social service agency personnel

- ◆ City planners, building permit inspectors, zoning personnel
- ◆ Mortgage brokers
- ◆ Professors (architecture, planning, real estate, housing)
- ◆ Administrators at the city or state department of housing finance
- ◆ Apartment finder services
- ◆ Roommate finder services
- ◆ HUD Section 8 administrators

> **Trend analysis helps you profitably adapt to change.**

Remember you want to discover demographic and psychographic trends, personal problems, shortages, and surpluses. Ask who's renting and who's buying where and why. Ask what's hot, what's not. When homeowners remodel, what features do they prefer? Are increasing (decreasing) numbers of people feeling financial pain?

Use Questionnaires

Years ago when I was in college promoting rock concerts with national and regional bands (another of my entrepreneurial quests), I needed to learn which bands would likely draw the biggest crowds. Following the principles that I was then learning in my marketing class, I developed a questionnaire and then asked local high school and college students to voice their preferences.

Since that first venture into survey research, I have used questionnaires dozens of times to better understand what tenants and homebuyers want, why they act the way they do, and how they plan to act. Although handing out and collecting surveys may not appeal to you, for $100 or so, you can probably hire a local college student to perform this research for you.

Focus Groups

During the past 20 years, focus groups have emerged as one of the most popular ways to get into the minds of potential tenants and homebuyers. To conduct a focus group, you merely bring together a sampling of people from your proposed target market; then, through give-and-take conversations, you probe their beliefs and feelings.

I suspect that nearly every major home and apartment builder in the country now runs focus groups to learn the thinking of their intended customers. To a certain degree, I ran my Stop Renting Now!™ seminars as a quasi-focus group. Real estate firms and mortgage lenders often paid my fees. In return, I provided these clients with the names of prospects along with the comments and concerns that I had elicited from my seminar's question and answer sessions.

In creating its Share-A-Home concept, Tropical Village, Inc., employed the Osceola [County] Council on Aging to hold 15 focus groups (more than 200 total participants). The insights that were gained helped Tropical Village formulate its marketing theme as well as the specific features, amenities, and services that the firm blended into its triplexes and total value proposition.

To take advantage of this research technique, you need not conduct a formal focus group. That probably stretches beyond the time, effort, and money that you want to put into your investment research—at least during your beginning stages. Nevertheless, if you find yourself (or can place yourself) in a group setting, try to get the group to focus on and discuss topics that could alert you to rental market opportunities. Entrepreneurial investors scout for profitable ideas everywhere they can find them.

Anticipate and Adapt to Change

Smart entrepreneurs also scout for change. They ask how evolving trends will affect the future demand for specific homes, apartments, neighborhoods, and communities.

The Age Wave

Everybody knows that the population is getting older. During the next 20 years, more than 60 million people will celebrate their 60th birthday. Sixty million new retirees are on the horizon. Where will these people want to live? What kinds of housing units will they want (Share-A-Homes)? What features will press their hot buttons?

The real estate investors who jump on the front end of this freight train to opportunity will certainly ride to glory. Yet, as I have emphasized, "over 60" itself doesn't define a target market *per se*. It merely flashes the signal to stop, look, and listen. What bull's eye segments within this over-60 market will remain underserved until some entrepreneur senses their need and creates a way to fill it? Here are some of the trends that demographers are beginning to detect.

> **What features appeal to "seniors?"**

1. **Downsizing.** A shift away from the McMansions that became so popular during the late 1980s and 1990s.
2. **College towns.** Retirees appreciate the combination of education, sports, arts, theater, and diversity without big city costs and aggravation.

3. **Rural/small towns.** Especially those that combine abundant outdoor recreation with a degree of upscale culture (such as Ashland, Oregon).

4. **Single-floor housing units.** Post-60 often prefer to avoid stairs.

5. **Doorways and door levers.** Wider doorways to accommodate wheelchairs and walkers. Door levers are easier to manage than doorknobs.

6. **Mild four-season climate.** While Florida will remain the most popular state for retirees, mild four-season states such as Tennessee, Georgia, the Carolinas, and Virginia will become increasingly popular. Also, Mississippi and Alabama will grow their in-migration of retirees.

7. **High cost to low cost areas.** Why live in a prewar Brooklyn bungalow when you can rent or own a large, new house or apartment just outside of sunny Orlando or Tampa for less than half the costs in Brooklyn?

8. **Security and low maintenance.** Lock and leave without worry. With extensive travel on the agenda, seniors won't want to concern themselves with what's happening to their home while they're away.

The previously mentioned trends represent just a sampling of senior trends to be expected. Stay tuned in for future developments.

Echo Boomers

Each year, thousands of articles discuss the effects that aging baby boomers will create for the housing market. But to date, the media have not spent much time on another perfectly predictable demographic trend.

The birth years for baby boomers were 1946–1964. The birth years for the baby bust were 1965–1977. Then beginning in 1978, annual births again started to climb into the 4 million a year range, and continued at or near that pace for more than 15 years.

The first of these so-called echo boomers will turn age 25 in 2003. Reminiscent of the 1970s, near record numbers of young people will once again be flooding into the entry-level housing market. What types of apartments, what features, what locations will appeal to the diverse segments of the echo generation? Put up your early detection antennae. Are the echo boomers sending you any signals as to how their preferences will evolve?

> **Near record numbers of young people will soon enter the rental market.**

Local Trends and Changes

The age wave and the echo boomers represent two definite and profound demographic changes that will hit full stride during the coming decade. Most importantly, how will these trends impact the areas where you plan to invest? Or vice-versa—can you discover areas (neighborhoods, communities) that will stand to benefit from the exploding growth of these two age groups?

What other demographic and psychographic trends are occurring in your investment area? When you talk with local housing experts and insiders, don't just dwell on the here and now. Explore their views about population and community change. Track shifts in tastes, age distribution, incomes, job growth, and neighborhood popularity. As they say in hockey, don't skate to where the puck is now; skate to where it's going.

> **Find a trend and ride it to profits.**

Plan to play into a trend. As the trend grows, so will your knowledge and ability. You will learn from your tenants. You will refine and expand your property purchase, property improvement, and rental strategy. Your profits will grow as the trend continues to roll along.

CHAPTER 6

Is the Property a Good Deal?

As an entrepreneurial investor who seeks superior returns, you will want to evaluate your properties according to multiple criteria. The key to making great deals lies in thinking through what the property will do for you, as well as what you can do for the property. Savvy investors work through their investment analysis using all of the following benchmarks:

- ◆ Replacement cost
- ◆ Per unit measures
- ◆ Gross rent multipliers
- ◆ Capitalized value
- ◆ Growth in equity
- ◆ Potential for creating value

After reviewing these value benchmarks, you'll see that even a below-market price may not yield the rate of return and margin of safety you would like. And contrary to popular belief, at times you can achieve a great return plus a margin of safety—even if you pay above market value.

The trick, of course, is to know what you're doing and why you're doing it. Too many investors simplistically jump after below-market buys, and reject in knee-jerk fashion all properties firmly priced above market. On closer inspection, either of these decision strategies may err.

How Much Would It Cost to Rebuild the Property?

When you invest in a property, you would like to profit as it appreciates in value. Over the long run, as construction costs go up and population increases, that's a safe forecast. In the short run, though, current market values sometimes jump too far above building costs. Eyeing large profits, builders rush to construct new houses, condominiums, and apartments. The market becomes glutted and then property prices and rents falter.

> **Over time, higher building costs pull up property values.**

The Construction Cycle

Here's how the construction cycle works: Typically, a city, town, or vacation area begins to "boom." Jobs and wages go up. More people move in. Interest rates decline. Apartment rents and home prices start to take off. Vacancies disappear. Inventories of unsold homes decline. Pretty soon, *existing* homes or apartments that could be built *new* for, say, $100,000 per unit begin to command values of say, $120,000, $130,000 or more.

Builders Spy Opportunity With market values of existing properties well above replacement costs, builders can quickly make a lot of money. Build at $100,000; sell at $130,000. Great! $30,000 profit. Unfortunately, in the past, too many builders have frequently rushed to meet the growing demand. Due to overly optimistic expectations, supply multiplies. A shortage becomes a surplus. Buyers who bought near the top of the cycle face disappointment (or worse) as rent levels and values temporarily stagnate or slide back to lower levels.

Recovery   Over time, builders pull back and gradually excess inventories diminish. Vacancies tighten, the inventory of unsold homes begins to fall, and potential renters again outnumber the supply of available properties. Property values and rents stabilize at first, but then edge up. Eventually, as shortages again loom on the horizon, vacancies dwindle. Prices take off on another short-term rapid run. The construction cycle turns another revolution.

Implications for Investors

The last major boom-bust construction cycle occurred in Texas in the mid to late 1980s. Properties that could be newly built for $75,000 to $100,000 sold for as much as $125,000 to $150,000. Condos and apartment projects, especially, multiplied with reckless abandon. Large real estate tax shelter benefits added fuel to the fire. Just as with the dot-coms and tech stocks, rapid price increases fed on themselves—until the bubble burst.

Pitfalls   Could investors have avoided getting caught in this downdraft? Absolutely. Had they kept an eye on construction costs, they could have anticipated problems. For whenever the market values of properties push more than 10 to 15 percent ahead of their replacement costs, the market is flashing yellow. Yet rather than cautiously slow down, most would-be investors (and builders) speed up. Savvy investors, though, pay attention to this warning sign. They back off from new acquisitions or buy only when they can get their price—not the inflated (and soon-to-be-deflated) market price.

> **Large profits for builders can bring too much new supply to market.**

The moral: Stay in touch with local builders or others who are in the know about contractor costs (building suppliers, lumber yards, appraisers, construction lenders). Or you might turn to one or more construction cost services. You can easily follow your local building costs through their manuals (at your library) or their Web sites. When builder profit margins grow ever fatter, oversupply will surely result.

Profit When Values Drop Below Costs   Rents low? Vacancies climbing? Unsold houses and condos piling up in the Realtors' Multiple Listing Service? Builders going bankrupt? Lenders foreclosing? Great! That's the perfect time for investors to buy—especially when market values end up below replacement costs because that means few builders will venture forth. Why pay more to build than you can get from a sale?

As long as emerging trends in the area point to a larger population, more jobs, a growing economic base, and a sought-after quality of life, prices (rents) are guaranteed to rise. More demand pressing against a relatively fixed total supply will reward investors with handsome returns.

Clean-Up Crews Earn Good Money   We frequently hear about the boom-bust cycles of real estate. But, in fact, the notorious (1980s–1990s) boom-busts of Texas, California, New York City, and several other areas do not reflect the norm. Housing markets in most areas remain far more stable. The odds are that you will never experience that kind of shakeout. While perhaps that's good in one sense, it's bad in another because clean-up crews can make stupendous returns. Consider the Reichmans, who marched into New York City during its 1974–1977 recession. Within a relatively few years their $300 million of office building acquisitions (primarily with borrowed money) carried a value in excess of $1 billion.

At the other end of the spectrum, a former student of mine in Dallas—whom I had taught at Southern Methodist University—bought his first investment during the down cycle of the early 1990s: a small foreclosed house for $8,000. After spending $2,500 for repairs and refurbishing (most of which he performed himself), he leased the house for $350 a month.

In buying during such hard times, did the Reichmans or my former student take a big risk? Not at all; in fact, quite the contrary!

> **Surplus markets reduce risk.**

The purchase prices of their properties lay so far below replacement costs that they were taking virtually no risk of any consequence. Both Dallas and New York City were (and remain) major capitals of industry and financial services. With their long-term growing base of jobs and population, a huge recovery in prices was only a matter of when, not if. In the meantime, the existing rents from the properties provided more than ample cash flows.

Have Money, Will Travel   Will similar local or regional shakeouts occur again? Probably. Although builders and construction lenders have supposedly entered a new era of disciplined building and lending, we've heard that story before. It seems that each generation forgets the mistakes of the past. They must relearn the lessons taught in earlier years.

> **Stay informed about out-of-town markets.**

Stay informed. Keep tabs on various cities and real estate markets around the country. Should property prices again plunge below their cost of replacement, don't miss that opportunity. Adopt the motto, "Have Money (Credit), Will Travel." If the bargains don't come to you, as an entrepreneurial investor, prepare yourself to go to the bargains.

Local (Regional) Recessions

Even without serious overbuilding, property prices can sometimes fall below replacement costs due to job declines and recession. During the early 1990s, large layoffs in defense and aerospace firms created the housing troubles of Southern California. Recall the "economic base" issues in Chapter 3. For now, though, just recognize that overbuilding and/or job losses can offer up grand opportunities to buy during a down cycle.

Market Value < Replacement Cost = Bargain Hunter's Delight

Per Unit Measures

Real estate investors often rely on various "per-unit" measures to help them decide whether a property looks like a good buy. Like

> **Quickly calculate per unit price comparisons.**

all "gross" or "rule-of-thumb" measures, per-unit figures signal whether a property *tends* to be priced over or under some benchmark norm. While never compelling on their own, these types of measures do provide meaningful benchmarks for investor comparisons.

Per Apartment Unit

When looking at multi-unit apartment buildings, you should divide the asking price by the number of apartment units in the property. For example, for an 8-unit property priced at $450,000, you would calculate:

$$\text{price per unit} = \frac{\$450,000}{8}$$

$$\text{price per unit} = \$56,250$$

If you know that other similar apartment buildings have typically *sold* for $60,000 to $70,000 per unit, you may have found a bargain. In addition, this and other "per" measures give you a quick way to compare prevailing prices when buildings differ in unit sizes. For example, say you're comparing six-unit, nine-unit, and eleven-unit properties at the respective prices of $275,000, $435,000, and $487,500. By figuring per-unit prices, you can more easily rank the properties from lowest to highest priced.

No. Units	Price	Price per Unit
11	$487,500	$44,318
6	$275,000	$45,833
9	$435,000	$48,333

Size, Quality and Location   Ideally, the units you compare should closely match each other; however, if that's not possible, adjust your valuations to reflect size, quality, and location differences among properties. Especially consider all of the location, site, and building features highlighted in Exhibit 5.1. I'm not trying to push you into the "analysis paralysis" so common in M.B.A. programs. But by trying to spot those "differences that make a difference," you can better judge properties according to their relative desirability and profit potential.

Buy in one market. Sell in another.	**Opportunity Knocks (Arbitrage)** Primarily, price-per-unit measures can help you find bargain buildings. But also, this measure can help you spot opportunities in two other ways:

1. **Size.** Change the size of the units from larger to smaller, or vice versa. Imagine that smaller 700 to 800 square-foot units sell and rent at substantial premiums over larger, 1,200 to 1,400 square-foot units. Thus, buying a building of predominantly larger units could pay off big when you reconfigure the building into one composed of smaller-sized units.

2. **Conversion.** You might also profit by noticing that buildings with two-bedroom rentals typically sell in the $40,000 to $50,000 per-unit range. In contrast, in similar condo buildings, two-bedroom units sell in the $70,000 to $80,000 range. Or, the price disparity could work in

the opposite direction. Either way, you may be able to buy at the lower-priced use, convert, then sell (or rent) at the high-priced use.

Although the previous types of arbitrage do not occur often, they do arise every now and then. By always paying attention to relative prices, the entrepreneurial investor stays poised to jump when this type of arbitrage opportunity knocks.

Per Square Foot (P.S.F.) Measures

You've probably heard property buyers and sellers refer to a house or other type of property by noting that it sold for, say, $135 per square foot. Price per square foot (p.s.f.) represents one of the most widely used methods of benchmark pricing. Investors and homebuyers alike rely on it to provide a ballpark measure of relative value. To calculate a per-square-foot figure, simply divide the total square footage of the unit (house, apartment, or total building) into its price:

$$\text{p.s.f.} = \frac{\text{asking price}}{\text{square footage}}$$

$$\text{p.s.f.} = \frac{\$285,000}{1,900}$$

$$\text{p.s.f.} = \$150$$

If "comp" sale properties typically have sold at $170–$180 p.s.f., you may have found a bargain at a price of $150 p.s.f.

Caveats If it were only so simple. As pointed out in Chapter 2, homebuyers and investors both go wrong using p.s.f. figures because no uniform standards apply to square foot measures. All square feet are not created equally in terms of quality, design, and usability. So calculate p.s.f. figures with caution. Unless designed and constructed with skill, converted garages, basements, and attics are worth far less per square foot than the functionally and aesthetically superior original living areas. Also, watch out for mismatches of size. Some buildings display room counts or room sizes far out of proportion to each other, or to competing properties.

I recently looked at a nearly new house (3,800 square feet) that included a *huge* great room, perhaps 800 or 900 square feet. Yet four of the home's five bedrooms were smallish, bland 10 × 12s, or so. The remainder of the home's square footage was primarily taken up by a *huge* master bedroom and a glorious "Roman" bath. You've probably seen houses like this one—several giant rooms for show, others dysfunctionally small. The house fails as an integrated living unit. Accordingly, this house eventually sold at $70 p.s.f. Other homes in the neighborhood typically fetched p.s.f. prices of $85 to $95. Use p.s.f. measures as a guide, but don't pay top-market prices for low-quality, ill-usable space.

> **Not all square footage counts equally.**

When I first began to buy apartments that had been converted from large houses, I failed to appreciate this point. Keep your critical senses tuned. Evaluate quality as well as quantity.

Land Value Caveat   When you look at p.s.f. pricing for existing properties, you'll find gross value figures. This type of p.s.f. includes the value of the building, the site improvements (fences, parking, decks, sidewalks, driveway), and the lot (land). As a rule-of-thumb benchmark, this technique works well—except when your comparable properties sit on sites that differ greatly in value.

For example, say you're checking p.s.f. prices and find a four-unit building that recently sold for around $450,000, or $89 per square foot. You find a similar four-unit property five blocks away. It's priced at a p.s.f. of $70. Have you found a bargain? Apparently so—until with a little more investigating, you learn that the lower-priced property sits within the boundaries of a higher crime area. As a result, its site is worth $50,000 less than the lots of the other quad that recently sold. Of course, relative to its rent levels and ap-

> **Always value the land separately from the building.**

preciation potential, this $70 p.s.f. quad still might make a good buy, but the p.s.f. price alone wouldn't tell you that. The lesson: Don't read too much, too soon into per-square-foot price comparisons. Always verify comparability of the property and location.

Replacement Costs   When investigating replacement costs (see preceding section), builders often quote construction costs in terms of price per square foot. Caveats apply here, too. Unlike comp sale p.s.f. figures, builder p.s.f. costs often exclude the value of the lot. Also, if you've ever built (or bought) a new house, you know that cost figures can differ dramatically. Not only will they differ among builders, but they will differ according to types of materials, the quality of the finishing, and the brand of the built-in appliances.

Before you apply a price per square foot construction cost figure to a property you're valuing, make sure you understand the precise nature of the estimate. In my area, the construction costs for newly built apartments range from a low of $60 p.s.f. up to more than $100 per square foot. As always, take care to match like for like.

Price Per Front Foot

Although popular as a pricing metric for retail sites, price per front foot plays a relatively small role in valuing residential properties. Chiefly, homebuyers or residential investors use it to benchmark waterfront sites. Because the most popular benefits of owning lakefront are views and beach area, the larger a site's shoreline, the greater its desirability, and the higher its value.

If waterfront is valued at $4,000 per front foot, a one-acre site with 125 feet of shoreline would sell at $500,000. If a site included only 80 feet of shoreline (other things equal), its value would equal $320,000. Of course, it's when "other things are *not* equal" that sometimes throws value estimates off track. But as a rule of thumb, price per front foot can convey a useful piece of information.

Gross Rent Multipliers (GRMs)

To value rental houses and small apartment buildings, investors frequently use annual or monthly gross rent multipliers (GRMs). An investor might check several comp sales and discover the following data:

	Annual Gross Rent	Sales Price	Annual GRM
College Terrace	$55,000	$434,500	7.9
Bivens Lake Apts.	$62,700	$526,680	8.4
Four Palms	$48,300	$323,610	6.7

If you find an income property with a relatively high GRM, it could signal either a price too high, or rents too low. Further checking would reveal the answer. Throughout the United States and Canada, I've seen annual GRMs as low as 4.0 (such as rundown properties or unpopular neighborhoods), and as high as 13 (coastal California cities). In my present university-dominated town, gross rent multipliers typically range from a low of 6.0 (unexceptional student housing) to 8.2 (newer units in professional, but not premier, neighborhoods.)

As a rule, when annual gross rent multipliers go much above 8.0, you're often looking at negative cash flows—unless you increase your down payment to 30 percent or more.[1] Because urban and vacation towns with high housing prices often produce GRMs of 10 or higher, income-oriented investors who live in those areas should buy their rental houses and apartments elsewhere. Alternatively, income-oriented investors in high-priced areas can look for neighborhoods or market niches (condominiums, lower-middle segment, outlying suburbs) that offer a better price/rent relationship.

> **High GRMs signal negative cash flow.**

---

1. Based on current mortgage rates for credit-worthy investors of around 6.0 to 7.0 percent on small income properties.

Capitalized Value

As another popular approach to value, most real estate investors use the following formula:

$$V = \frac{NOI}{R}$$

Where "V" represents the estimated market value of the property; NOI (net operating income) represents the property's rents less expenses; and R equals the market capitalization rate. Essentially, this formula is the real estate investor's version of the price/earnings (P/E) ratio that is used by stock market investors. To illustrate, here's how this technique would look for a six-unit apartment building:

Income Statement (Annual)

1.	Gross annual potential rents ($725 × 6 × 12)	$52,200
2.	Income from parking and storage areas	5,062
3.	Vacancy and collection losses @ 7%	(4,009)
4.	Effective gross income	$53,254

Less operating and fixed expenses

5.	Trash pick-up	$1,080
6.	Utilities	450
7.	Licenses and permit fees	206
8.	Advertising and promotion	900
9.	Management fees @ 6%	3,195
10.	Maintenance and repairs	3,000
11.	Yard care	488
12.	Miscellaneous	2,250
13.	Property taxes	3,202
14.	Property and liability insurance	1,267
15.	Reserves for replacement	1,875
	Total operating and fixed expenses	$17,914
16.	Net operating income (NOI)	$35,340

Calculating NOI looks relatively straightforward. If you're not careful, though, you can err in several ways. To alert you to these possible traps, think about the following caveats and explanations (which match up numerically with the entries shown on the income statement):

1. **Gross potential rents.** For this figure, use the property's existing rent levels; if its current rents sit above market, use market rent levels. Verify all leases for rental amounts and lease terms. Do not use a rent figure based on your anticipated rent increases (if any).

2. **Extra income.** With many properties you can charge for rental application fees, parking, storage, laundry, party room, garages, and so on. Verify all such existing income. Don't project extra income that's not been proven by past operating experience or reasonable market data.

3. **Vacancy and collection losses.** Use market vacancy rates, or the current owner's vacancies for the past year—whichever is *higher*. Also, when judging "market" vacancy rates, take your figures from the market niche in which this property currently operates. Vacancy rates may vary significantly by location, apartment size, quality, and rent level. As you compare vacancy rates by market niche, try to spot those segments that are experiencing the greatest shortages.

4. **Effective gross income.** It is from this cash that you will pay property expenses and mortgage payments. If you overestimate rent levels or underestimate vacancies, you may end up cash short.

5. **Trash pick-up.** Verify rates and permissible quantities. Look for lower-cost alternatives.

6. **Utilities.** In addition to common area lighting, some buildings include centralized heat and air systems. Verify the amounts of these expenses with utility companies. (Personal note: I would never again operate a building where apartment units lacked individual HVAC units— unless the building price was extremely low or the HVAC system extremely efficient. Most older centralized sys-

tems seldom distribute heat and air conditioning uniformly. Tenants persistently voice complaints of too cold or too hot.)

7. **License and permit fees.** On occasion, owners of rental properties are required to pay municipal fees of one sort or another.

8. **Lease-up expenses.** Ideally, you will generate a good supply of rental applicants from free postings, referrals, and inquiries; otherwise, you may need to advertise. Also, you'll probably need to pay for credit checks on potential tenants.

9. **Management fees.** Even if you self-manage your units, allocate some expense here for your time and effort. Don't confuse return on labor for return on investment.

10. **Maintenance and repairs.** Ditto. Enter an expense to pay yourself or others. "I'll take care of that myself" shouldn't mean, "I'll work for free."

11. **Grounds maintenance.** Yard care entails mowing the lawn, trimming hedges, removing snow, cleaning up leaves, tending to the flower beds, and so on.

12. **Miscellaneous.** You will incur such odds-and-ends expenses as lease preparation, auto mileage, and long-distance telephone charges.

13. **Property taxes.** Verify amount, tax rate, and assessed value. Check accuracy. Note whether the property is subject to any special assessments (sewer, sidewalks, water reclamation).

14. **Property and liability insurance.** Verify exact coverage for property and types of losses. Increase deductibles and limits on liability.

15. **Reserves for replacement.** Eventually, you'll need to replace the roof, HVAC, appliances, carpeting, and other limited-life items. Allocate a pro rata annual amount here.

16. **Net operating income (NOI).** Subtract all expenses from effective gross income. You now have the numerator for $V = NOI/R$.

As a general principle, entrepreneurial investors first use a conservative approach to figuring out a building's NOI. They don't

Ask for the seller's Schedule E.

make grand assumptions about potential rent increases. They don't omit necessary expenses. They try to verify and double check all expense figures. They charge for their own labor (if any); and they allocate reasonable amounts for replacement reserves. In addition, you'll ask to see the sellers' Schedule E where they have reported property revenues and expenses to the IRS. (You may get resistance on this request, but carefully weigh the sellers' response.)

Estimate Market Value

To calculate value via the capitalized income approach, you next need to come up with an appropriate capitalization rate (R). Essentially, this rate represents your unleveraged, pre-tax annual cash return, just as the dividend yield represents your unleveraged, annual cash return on stocks. Fortunately for real estate investors, the cap rate (R) for income properties typically towers over the now diminutive dividend yield for stocks.

Calculate R   You calculate a market capitalization rate by comparing the NOIs (net operating incomes) of similar properties to their respective selling prices. To come up with this type of infor-

Cap rates are set by local markets.

mation, you can talk with competent realty agents who regularly sell (and preferably own) rental properties, other investors (from a local realty investment club, for example), property management firms who also handle sales, and property owners who have recently sold. People in real estate (generally) tend to help each other and share information. In terms of format, you would display these market data as follows:

Property	Recent Sales Price	NOI	R
Hampton Apts. (8 units)	$452,900	$43,211	9.54%
Woodruff Apts. (6 units)	360,000	35,900	9.97
Adams Manor (6 units)	295,000	28,440	9.6
Newport Apts. (9 units)	549,000	53,170	9.78
Ridge Terrace (8 units)	471,210	42,409	9.0

From the various comparable property cap rates (R), you would select those buildings and locations most comparable to the property you're evaluating, say 9.0 to 9.5 percent. You would then calculate a market value range for the property you're appraising as follows:

$$1. \quad V = \frac{\$35,340 \ (NOI)}{.09 \ (R)}$$

$$V = \quad \$392,666$$

$$2. \quad V = \frac{\$35,340 \ (NOI)}{.098 \ (R)}$$

$$V = \quad \$360,612$$

Throughout the country, cap rates for small rental properties may run from as low as 6 or 7 percent up to 12, 14 percent, or higher. Generally, a *low* cap rate occurs when you're valuing highly desirable properties in good to top neighborhoods. Relatively high cap rates tend to follow less desirable properties in so-so neighborhoods. Apartment buildings with condo conversion potential also tend to sell with low cap rates. Remember, a low cap rate translates into a relatively high value; and a high cap rate produces a relatively low value.

> **The lower the cap rate, the higher the value.**

If you find that across all types of properties and neighborhoods in your city, cap rates in your area are too low (i.e., prices too high), search other areas. Low cap rates (lower earnings multiples) typically offer lower risk and higher cash-on-cash returns.

P/E Ratio Analogy   Stock market investors may see the parallel between cap rates and P/E ratios. If a property sells with a cap rate of .085 (8.5 percent), that figure would represent a P/E multiple of close to twelve. Or conversely, a stock with a P/E multiple of, say, 14 would show an earnings yield (cap rate) of 7.1 percent (.071). Either way, these similar techniques both try to show the relative valuation of a stream of income. With stocks, a stream of corporate earnings; with real estate, a stream of rental earnings.

Likewise, over time these yields will move up or down according to the strength of the economy, the outlook for interest rates, the potential for higher rents, the quality of the income, and various risk factors. No single cap rate can ever represent the "correct" rate. You must always investigate the relevant submarket.

Anticipate the Future; Pay for the Present

In the previous example, you would have relied on *verified* income and expense figures drawn from the property's current operating history and your knowledge of competitive properties. Yet, as an entrepreneurial investor, you will make changes to the property through improvements, better management, and perhaps even neighborhood revitalization. These three changes can dramatically boost net income and at the same time lower the property's cap rate. Your property's value can quickly jump by 20 percent, 30 percent, or more.

> **Sellers will ask you to pay for potential. Investors pay only for the present.**

So, here's where you need to exercise caution. When negotiating to buy, focus on the present, not your (or the seller's) vision of the future. Investors who anticipate great profits often pay too much. They let the sellers capture the value potential that they plan to create.

Reason and Judgment   When you buy conservatively, you enhance your margin of safety. On occasion, though, you may run across a super property at a relatively high price. Should you automatically reject it? Not necessarily. But before you buy, check, verify, and recheck your optimistic expectations. Sometimes a "fully valued" property with extraordinary potential will outperform a bargain-priced property with very limited upside.

When you do buy high, be wary of the risks you're taking. Unnoticed perils have brought down many a sure thing. Does your market data on the local economy, your target tenants, and competing properties (rents, features) truly support your plans to grow the property's NOI.

Mum's the Word   Novice investors, especially, tend to give away too much of their plans for a property. To buy at a conservative price, don't turn your cards so that the sellers (or their sales agent) can see them. If you explicitly question the sellers in ways that reveal your value-creating ideas, the sellers will likely use that potential to strengthen their own negotiating position. In most cases sellers already hold inflated ideas about all the great things you can do to enhance their property—which regrettably, they say, they never had the time (or money) to accomplish. With such ploys common, you need not load the sellers with even more ammunition to fire back at you. As much as possible, focus your negotiations on the present. Retain the future as a bonus for your entrepreneurial talents and insights.

> **Avoid signaling your plans to a seller.**

Cash-on-Cash Return

Many investors judge their properties by the cash-on-cash rate of return they can achieve. As a result, investors scrutinize the cost and terms of their financing as much as they do a property. To illustrate, let's bring forward that six-unit apartment building from several pages back. Assume you can buy that property for $350,000, or just under $60,000 per unit. You talk to a lender and tentatively arrange a mortgage for $280,000 (an 80 percent loan-to-value ratio). The lender wants an 8.0 percent interest rate with a 25-year term. You would need to come up with $70,000. Here are the relevant figures:

Loan amount	$350,000
Annualized mortgage payments @ 8.0%; 25 years	25,932
Net operating income (NOI)	35,340
Less mortgage payments	25,932
BTCF (before tax cash flow)	9,408

$$\text{Cash-on-cash return} = \frac{\text{BTCF}}{\text{Down payment}}$$

$$= \frac{\$9,408}{\$70,000}$$

$$= 13.44\%$$

Not bad. But say your hurdle rate equals 15 percent. What might you do to boost your cash-on-cash return? For starters, you could try to get the lender to extend the loan term to 30-years. If successful, your annualized payments (assuming no change in interest rate) would drop to $24,652; therefore, BTCF would increase to $10,688 (35,340 – 24,652):

$$\text{Cash-on-cash return} = \frac{\$10,688}{\$70,000}$$

$$= 15.3\%$$

If you don't like extending the loan term to 30-years, you could try to push the lender down to a 7.625 percent interest rate. In that case, your annualized mortgage payments (25 years) would total $25,102. Your BTCF would equal $10,237 (35,340 – 25,102):

$$\text{Cash-on-cash return} = \frac{\$10,237}{70,000}$$

$$= 14.28\%$$

Oops, that lower rate won't quite do it. But as an enterprising investor, you've got a number of other options:

1. Try for an even lower interest rate (7.5 percent would work)
2. Ask the seller to take back an interest only balloon note for five years at 7.0 percent for, say, $20,000.
3. Negotiate a lower price for the property.
4. Switch from a 25-year, fixed-rate mortgage to a 7.0 percent 5/20 adjustable-rate mortgage. This tactic would work especially well if you planned to sell (or exchange) the property within five years.
5. Look for reasonable and certain ways to boost the property's net income. Increase rent collections, raise occupancy. Cut expenses. (See following chapters.)
6. Agree to pay the seller a higher price in exchange for owner financing on terms more favorable (lower interest rate, lower down payment) than a bank would offer.

> **You find a property. You negotiate and structure a good deal.**

Any or all of these techniques *could* work. You would just have to experiment with the numbers and negotiate for some mutually agreeable solution. The point is that as an investor in real estate, the "market" never provides you a return. You provide your own return based upon the price, terms of financing, property improvements, and market strategy that you put together.

Growth in Equity

In addition to a bargain price and annual cash flows, you will also see your real estate wealth growth through property appreciation and mortgage amortization (paying back the amount you borrow with the rents you collect). Together, appreciation and amortization turn acorns (small down payments) into oak trees (equity that multiplies 5, 10, 20 times, or more). To see this wealth-building power of income properties, look at Figure 6.1.

For purposes of illustration, say you buy a $400,000 fourplex and finance it with a 90 percent loan at 6.5 percent interest for 25 years. You think this property will appreciate at a minimum rate of 3 percent a year, but that it could increase in value by as much as 7 percent a year. Under this range of assumptions, you can see that after just five years, your original equity of $40,000 will grow to at least $138,343. And at an appreciation rate of 7 percent, your equity after five years would reach $240,743.

Study these amounts of equity growth very closely. You can't help to realize that a huge multiplication of original equity does not require heroic assumptions about the rate of appreciation. Rather, the figures reveal the enormous power of leverage.

Now for further comparison, assume that instead of buying this small income property, you invested your $40,000 in stocks and earned a 10 percent net rate of return. Here's how your $40,000 would grow:

Stock Returns @ 10 Percent

Today	5 Years	10 Years	15 Years	25 Years
$40,000	$56,000	$108,280	$178,120	$482,240

Even when you contrast your stock market wealth to the equity you could earn with just 3 percent per year of property appreciation, the property wealth wins by a long shot. (And we haven't even considered the positive annual cash flows you'll receive as your rent collections increase over the years.)

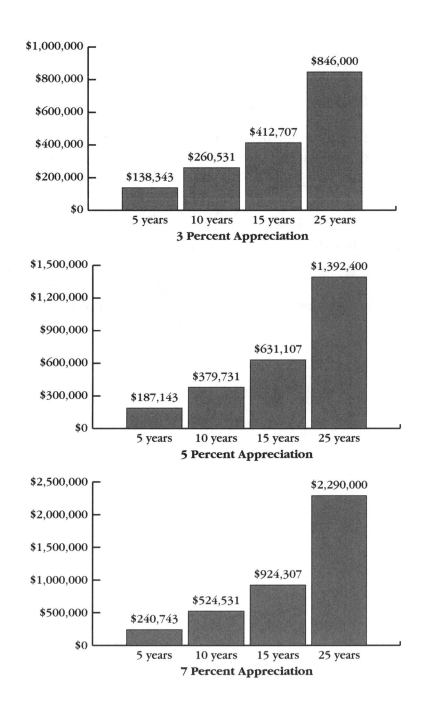

Figure 6.1 Growing Original Equity of $40,000 under Varying Rates of Property Appreciation.

Don't Settle for Low Rates of Appreciation

But here's even better news. As an entrepreneurial property investor, you need not settle for property appreciation rates of just 3, 5, or even 7 percent. Unlike stocks, you can use your entrepreneurial skills to study the market, improve the property, develop a competitive edge for your target market, and locate communities and neighborhoods that are poised to "beat the market." Any or all of these efforts will accelerate your gains in equity. With that said, we now turn to show you how to achieve these superior results.

> **Create your own appreciation.**

Collect More Rents

Think back to the basic value formula we discussed in Chapter 6:

$$V = \frac{NOI \text{ (Net Operating Income)}}{R \text{ (Capitalization Rate)}}$$

You will boost the value of a property anytime you can figure out a way to either increase the numerator (NOI) or decrease the denominator (R) of this equation. To illustrate: Assume that you find a six-unit property currently yielding an NOI of $48,000 a year. Based on talks with real estate agents, other investors, and several appraisers, you figure this property "as is" should sell with a cap rate of 9 percent (.09). Accordingly, you calculate the "as is" value of these six units at $533,333.

$$533,333 \ V = \frac{48,000 \text{ (NOI)}}{.09 \text{ (R)}}$$

If you're negotiating with a motivated seller (as opposed to an owner who's just "testing the market"), you should be able to buy this property for a price of around $525,000, give or take depending on terms and conditions. If you did nothing but keep these units rented and the property adequately maintained, you would enjoy those 3 to 7 percent a year average rates of appreciation that most investors experience.

Never Accept Average

If you're happy with those kinds of average appreciation rates, sit back, hire a caretaker apartment manager, and collect your rent checks without work or worry. But I urge you not to accept average. If you really want to get on the fast track for building wealth, study the market and put on your entrepreneurial thinking hat. By making changes that will boost the property's NOI by just 10 percent and drop your R to 8.5 percent, you will jump the value of this property to $621,176—immediate gain in equity of $87,843 ($621,176 less $533,333):

$$\$632,176 \ = \ \frac{\$52,800 \text{ (new NOI)}}{.085 \text{ (new R)}}$$

> **Become a value creator.**

Are such large increases in value possible within, say, a period of 6 to 12 months? Absolutely! Why? Because most owners of small income properties still think of themselves as "landlords" (with emphasis on "m' lord"); and, they think of their residents merely as "renters" (vassals) with all of the pejorative connotation that word can imply.

In addition, as I emphasize many times over, most small investors do not intelligently survey competing properties, nor do they try to persistently adapt their market strategies to resident needs, wants, and preferences. To speak of a PVP (preferred value proposition) or target marking to these owners would get you a "what the heck are you talking about" look. I cannot believe the number of owners of small income properties who still think that they're operating in feudal times.

Stand Out and Stand Above

Never think of yourself as a landlord. Never define what you do as "owning rental properties." Instead, think of yourself as providing

> **Never become a landlord.**

your customers with a product (housing) that stands out and above your competitors. I guarantee that if you adopt this attitude, your profits will shoot far above average for two reasons:

1. **Better resident relations.** The residents of your properties will reward you with lower turnover, higher rents, and fewer problems.
2. **Alert to opportunities.** With a customer-oriented, constant-improvement attitude, you will consistently look for and come up with ideas that will add value to your property operations.

A Strategy of Your Own

Good management and marketing depend on continued study of competing properties and resident preferences. No one can tell you the specific strategy that will yield *you* the highest profits. Certainly, you can read a dozen (or more) books on "landlording" and most of them will give you a precise list of dos and don'ts that may cover everything from rental applications to waterbeds. While ideas from these books can often prove suggestive, never accept them as the final word.

What works today may not work tomorrow. What works in Peoria may not go over in Paducah. What works in a tight rental market may prove less effective in a high-vacancy market. What works best with HUD Section 8 tenants may actually turn away those upscale residents of your more expensive buildings. Should you accept pets, smokers, or college students? It all depends.

In principle, you always want to offer your selected segment of renters the value proposition that they will prefer—yet, at the same time, a value proposition that fattens your bottom line. In actual practice, you can find that profit-maximizing value proposition only through market study and experimentation.

In this and the following chapters, I will share with you many pointers that you might try to beef up your NOI and lower the cap rate that future buyers (other investors) will apply to your properties. But in keeping with my overall theme, recognize that no one can know precisely what will work best:

♦ For you
♦ In your market
♦ For the types of properties you will own
♦ For the types of tenants that you would like to attract
♦ With respect to your personal resources (time, money, effort, imagination)

> **Keep experimenting to consistently improve.**

Nevertheless, if you keep an alert attitude, an open mind, and a never-ending desire to learn and increase your knowledge, I am absolutely certain that you won't merely build wealth with small income properties—you will do so at a very quick pace.

Verify Current Rent Collections

When you begin to shop for income properties, you must accurately assess the "as is" value of the property; otherwise, you risk overpaying. But that task isn't really as easy as Chapter 6 leads you to believe. For in fact, your need for personal and intelligent analysis is heightened in the field of income properties (relative to single-family houses) not only because each multi-unit property stands unique to all others, but also because owners and their sales agents rarely tell you everything they know about their properties. If you are expecting full and accurate disclosure, sorry, you're dreaming.

<table>
<tr><td>

Truth, lies, and income statements.

</td><td>

As a matter of law and practice, sellers in this market are held to lower standards of truthfulness. Before individual investors (buyers) can claim in court that they've been duped by a seller's misrepresentations or nondisclosures, such buyers generally must show that they complied with their legal "duty to investigate."

</td></tr>
</table>

In fact, nearly all property income statements, fliers, and sales brochures will include a disclaimer similar to the following:

> The information herein has been obtained from sources believed reliable. While we do not doubt its accuracy, we have not verified it and make no guarantee, warranty, or representation about it. It is your responsibility to independently confirm its accuracy and completeness. Any projections, opinions, assumptions, or estimates used are for example only and do not represent the current or future performance of the property. The value of this transaction to you depends on tax and other factors which should be evaluated by your tax, financial, and legal advisors. You and your advisors should conduct a careful, independent investigation of the property to determine to your satisfaction the suitability of the property for your needs.

Essentially, this disclaimer means that you're on your own. No matter what the sellers or their sales agent tells you about a property's past (or future) rent collections (and expenses), you still must conduct your own "careful, independent investigation." Therefore, to verify an owner's currently reported rent collections, adopt the following techniques.

Examine All Leases and Rental Applications

When you look through the leases, you will want to learn the names of all current residents, the rental rates for each unit, the lease expi-

Closely examine the rent roll.

ration dates, the amounts of deposits, whether the owner provided rent concessions, and any supplementary payments for, say, pets, parking, or extra tenants. From the lease applications, if the seller will show them to you, you can try to determine the creditworthiness of the tenants, their places of employment, and the period of time each tenant has lived in the building.

Interpreting the Rental Information

Overall, this information will help you get a more in-depth (and perhaps more accurate) view of both the quality and quantity of rental revenues. For example, you could find that a high percentage of tenants have moved into the building only recently; they posted small security deposits; they tend to work in unstable jobs; and they exhibit credit scores that are scraping bottom. Obviously, a tenant mix of this caliber will typically result in higher turnover, larger collection losses, and not unlikely, more damages to the property due to lack of care. Almost certainly, these tenants will not provide the amount of rent collections or net operating income that the owner claims. Discount accordingly.

On the other hand, you might find a building with a resident mix of strongly qualified long-term tenants who have posted large security deposits as well as deposits for their last month's rents. In addition, the owners of this property show you a bona fide waiting list. In this case, not only does the owners' reported rent collections seem reliable, but (as we discuss later in this chapter) you may have found a building that could maintain low vacancies even at significantly higher rent levels.

Rent Collections, Not Rental Rates

Too many new investors merely accept the owner's rent figures and then subtract that ubiquitous 5 percent vacancy factor. In

> **It's not how much you charge; it's how much you collect.**

truth, many property owners do not *collect* 95 percent of their scheduled rents—even if they achieve 95 percent occupancy. So, Step 1, to verify rents, verify the lease rates the tenants have agreed to pay. Step 2, realistically estimate vacancy and collection losses. Your profits, and the building's value, rest upon bankable funds, not leaky leases.

Talk with Tenants

Prior to buying a small income property, I always talk with a sampling of the building's tenants. This practice serves four purposes.

◆ Identify problems in the building.
◆ Identify problems with tenants.
◆ Verify lease and application data.
◆ Generate ideas for improvement.

Problems in the Building   "Not enough parking." "Too much noise." "The bills for heat and air are outrageous—$277 last month." "These walls are paper thin." "This place lacks security. We've had three break-ins during the past six months." "The closets in this apartment are too small, and there's no place for long-term storage." "No place to park or store my bicycle." "Cockroaches, ugh. This place is crawling with cockroaches."

> **Ask tenants, "What is it that you like least about living here?"**

To really learn about a building, talk with the tenants. This question nearly always elicits a response, "Tell me, what don't you like around here." Of course, sometimes the tenants will speak well of the building (or its owner). But more often they like to complain. They frequently hesitate to say good things because those kinds of comments could lead to an increase in rents.

Some sellers attach a "please do not disturb the tenants" to their advertising or promotional flyer. While I do not "disturb" the tenants, I would never let that statement deter me from talking with them.

Problems with Tenants   Bad tenants can ruin a potentially good building. If some tenants create hassles (or worse) for others, then you want to know about it before you structure your offer to buy the property. Problems within a property *and* problems with disruptive tenants can adversely impact vacancies, turnover, and rent collections.

Verify Lease and Application Data   On occasion, leases and application data do not portray the true facts about a property's tenants. At times, sellers actually have created phantom leases with false data. Absent outright fraud, though, your talks with tenants might reveal rent concessions that aren't recorded in the written file that you were given to review. You might also find some units are being sublet or are otherwise occupied by residents who aren't on the lease and may never have completed a rental application. Before you buy, you want to put together a rent roll that's as accurate as possible. Otherwise, both your NOI and cap rate (risk rate) figures may err.

Generate Ideas for Improvement   Whenever you shop a building, you want to divide the "problems" you find into two piles: economically unsolvable, and opportunity laden. As your talks with tenants reveal the strengths and weaknesses of the "as is" property, you're valuing it as it stands today. But you're also thinking how you might profitably improve it tomorrow. Through the eyes of a critical buyer, you itemize its faults and profit-draining negatives. Through the eyes of an entrepreneurial investor, you visualize ways to turn lead into gold.

> **Tenants will give you ideas for profitable improvements.**

Your Competitive Market Analysis

You will always check the rent data an owner gives you against the rent levels of the competitive units that you've looked at. "You say you're getting $850 a month for your two-bedrooms? That's interesting. I haven't found any other 2/2s in the neighborhood that are asking over $775 a month. How do you attract renters who will pay $850?"

You may not want to state your inquiry quite so bluntly, but you can't expect to negotiate a reasonable price for the property if the sellers hold illusions about the rental value of their units. On the other hand, maybe the building does include some attributes that warrant higher rents. (Though personally, I would typically hesitate to buy a property at the top end of a neighborhood rent range. With fully priced rent rates, your ability for upside is heavily anchored.)

Leases or not, in the final analysis, it is your knowledge of the market that will adequately inform you about the amount of rent collections that you can expect a property to yield in its current physical condition and management practices. Likewise, to estimate rent collections after improvements, ignore sellers' puffery—"All you need to do is paint and recarpet these units. You can easily get another $150 a month. I would have done it myself, but I've just been too busy at the restaurant I own." Maybe the seller's right, but you won't know for sure until you've actually visited and inspected a fair sampling of competing properties.

> **The market, not leases, will tell you the rental value of the units.**

Set Your Rents with Market Savvy

Many owners of small income properties devote far too little effort to figuring out the rental rates that they should charge for their units. They underprice. They overprice. They don't make rent-enhancing improvements. They fail to adequately segment their tenants. They spend too much money on ineffective advertising, and too little on target marketing. If they experience high vacancies, they blame a soft market. If they experience extremely low vacancies, they pride themselves on their skill as a landlord.

All in all, these mistakes (and many others) flow from the same source. Property owners just don't realize the great profits they're missing because they set their rents to reflect their own personal whim or arbitrary judgment—rather than market reality.

Say you own a 12-unit building. You underprice by $25 a month. The applicable cap rate is .09 (9 percent). How much does this error cost you?

$$\text{Lost income} = \$25 \times 12 \text{ units} \times 12 \text{ months}$$

$$= \$3,600 \text{ per year}$$

$$\text{Lost building value} = \frac{\$3,600}{.09}$$

$$= \$40,000$$

And those losses accrue when underpricing by just $25 per unit per month! Move that pricing error up to $50 or $100 a month, and your losses for that 12-unit property shoot up into the range of $100,000 to $200,000. Make no mistake. Underpriced rents can cost you a bundle of money. Overpricing, too, can also cost you plenty in terms of vacancies, turnovers, high advertising costs, low prospect conversion rates, property damage, and bad debts. Before you set your rent rates, think through your decision with analytical rigor. You will gain large rewards for your effort.

The Myth of "Market" Rent Levels

If apartments were a homogeneous good, such as cans of Campbell's tomato soup or bottles of Coca Cola, you could

> **Consider a market rent range, not *the* market rate.**

rightly expect every apartment to rent for the same price. You might talk meaningfully about a "market" rent level. But, in fact, apartment buildings and their individual units differ in dozens of ways that their potential tenants find appealing or unappealing:

- Views
- Energy usage/efficiency
- Square footage
- Natural light
- Ceiling height
- Quiet/noisiness
- Parking
- Room count
- Appliances (quality, quantity)
- Landscaping
- Quality of finishes
- Heat/air conditioning
- Decks/patios/balconies
- Cleanliness
- Carpeting/floor coverings
- Electrical outlets
- Emotional appeal
- Color schemes/aesthetics
- Living area floor plan
- Closet space
- Storage space
- Kitchen functionality
- Kitchen pizzazz
- Entryway convenience
- Tenant demographics
- Tenant lifestyles, attitudes
- Lighting
- Security
- Laundry facilities
- Fireplace
- Physical condition
- Window coverings
- Types/style of windows
- Image/reputation

And this list doesn't even address other important items such as the amount of the security deposit (total move-in cash), the terms of the lease, the quality of the management, and last, but far from least, the multiple attributes of location. We shall deal with each of these issues in due course, but the principal point is this: You can't intelligently say that your two-bedroom, two-bath units should rent for $675 a month—until you've compared your units feature-by-feature to competitive units.

Rent Levels and Vacancy Rates

Assume that you survey four similar competitive 16-unit buildings (all units 900 sq. ft., 2/2s). You discover the following rents:

	Two Bedrooms	Number of Vacancies
Building No. 1	$600	0
Building No. 2	$650	1
Building No. 3	$725	3
Building No. 4	$750	4

Other things equal, the higher the rent, the higher the vacancies and turnover.

In the real world, of course, you're not likely to find four perfectly comparable buildings. But I've structured this example simply to make you see that "low" rents typically lead to low vacancies. "High" rents typically lead to high vacancies. So, if by chance you look only at the rent levels in Building No. 3 and No. 4, you might erroneously conclude a "market" rent of around $725 to $750. In fact, though, after you match the vacancy rate to the rent rate, you see that both of these owners are probably overpricing their units.

The Myth of the "Market" Vacancy Rate

I've talked with property owners who have told me something like this: "I'm not going to increase rents this year. The market's too soft. The Realtor's Association is reporting a market vacancy rate of almost 8 percent. I don't want to give my tenants a reason to move out in this type of competitive free-for-all."

In one sense, these owners are displaying market awareness, but they're not displaying market savvy. Although it's true that too many owners do try to raise rents in soft markets and end up with high vacancies and turnover, before you actually forego the rent increase, look at the market data more closely. Seldom do vacancies spread themselves equally among all locations, types of units, and price ranges. I've seen situations where a "market" vacancy rate in a mid-size town shot up because of serious management/tenant problems in several large HUD projects.

Absent that type of anomaly, vacancy rates still may cluster within certain segments of the overall market, while demand for

> **What does "market" really refer to?**

other types of units remain brisk. For example, in my city, apartment rentals above $1,000 per month are meeting substantial resistance because $1,000 a month will finance a reasonably nice house at today's interest rates (at the prevailing home prices in my area). Middle-income renters are asking themselves, "Why rent when we can own?" Yet, within the $400 to $650 a month price range, the vacancy rate still sits below 4 percent.

The moral: Never accept "market" rent figures, nor "market" vacancy figures without first breaking those figures down by market segments. You want to find out the what, where, who, and why of those numbers before you rely on them for your rent-setting decisions.

Think Rent Range, Not Rent Rate

Whenever you survey rents, you develop a more informative picture when you think rent range. Try to compare each rental price with both the features and the vacancy factors within a building. Look for points of market resistance. Look for the low end of what's available. In any city, you will always find a range of rents among somewhat comparable apartments. Sometimes you can explain these variances in terms of unit size, quality, or vacancy rates, but sometimes units are simply underpriced. Their rents sit well below the amounts the apartments could command—even in "as is" condition.

Raise Rents without Substantially Improving the Building

When you first take ownership of a building, you must abide by the terms of the lease that the previous owners have signed with the current tenants. If a lease still has six months to run at $625 a month, you can't arbitrarily raise the rent. You can, however, raise rents as vacancies occur, as lease renewals come up, and through renegotiation of existing leases. Also, you might find buildings where many current tenants signed a one-year lease when they moved into the building two or three years ago, but now stay on an informal month-to-month tenancy. With 30-day notice (or as otherwise specified by state or local law), you can raise the rents on these tenants.

> **Rent increases can immediately boost NOI, hence building value.**

Confirm Your Suspicions

As an investor in small income properties, you will always try to keep a sharp eye out for properties with low rents relative to comparable competing units. They're like finding a pile of $1,000 bills.

But how do you confirm your suspicion? Say your market survey leads you to believe that the units would fill up at a higher rent level, but you want more evidence. Here's what to look for:

1. **Waiting lists.** Some property owners (managers) take great pride in their waiting lists. They display their waiting lists as a badge of honor. In fact, more than anything else (except in tight rent-controlled cities), a long waiting list typically signals below market rents.
2. **Zero vacancies.** "We never have a vacancy. These units always rent the first day." Rents are probably too low.
3. **High conversion rate.** "These units rent fast. The first person who looks at one of our apartments nearly always takes it." Low rents probably explain why.

4. **Low turnover rate.** "We seldom have a vacancy. Many of our tenants have been with us for years." Wonder why?

5. **Tenant improvements.** "Our maintenance costs are very low. Our tenants are always fixing up their apartments and taking care of things themselves. We rarely hear any complaints." Tenants with low rents seldom make a nuisance of themselves. They prefer to maintain a low profile.

If you can find a building at a reasonable price where you hear these types of comments, buy it! You can almost certainly raise the rents—even without making any substantial improvements to the property.

Why Owners Underprice Their Units

Owners underprice their apartment units for one or more of the following reasons:

- **Low hassle.** It's certainly easier to own a building that stays rented with complacent tenants.
- **Market ignorance.** Few owners actually perform competitive market surveys. Instead, they rely on hearsay, intuition, and general news about vacancy rates, the economy, and inflation.
- **Charity.** "Many of our tenants live on fixed incomes. We wouldn't feel right forcing them to move by raising their rents."
- **No mortgage.** Many long-term property owners bought their buildings when property prices were much lower. They have now paid off (or paid down) their mortgage balances. Owners such as these feel no pressure to raise their rents. No alligators are chewing on them.

Do any of these reasons make economic sense? Not usually. Yet, over and over throughout my career, I've seen owners under-manage their properties in ways that fail to maximize their rent collections. Sure, every owner wants low turnover, complacent tenants, and quick rent-ups when vacancies do occur. But at what cost? That's the real issue. Experience shows that these owners give up too much for too little. With an improved management and market strategy, you don't need to give away your units to keep them rented.

Investor Opportunities with Stage-of-Life Sellers

> **Win-win with seller financing.**

I particularly like to find buildings owned by older persons who now suffer burnout. After years of intensive hands-on management, they want relief. To achieve this goal, they purposely charge low rents. In turn, they reap the rewards of low hassle, low turnover, and low vacancy. But they give up substantial cash flow.

So, here's where you can profit. Offer to buy their property at its "as is" value with seller financing. In most cases, the mortgage payments you make will actually increase the amount of money these owners have been putting in their pocket each month.

A Look at the Numbers   In other words, if the owners currently rent out the property to bring in gross rents of, say, $32,000 per year before expenses, these owners are pocketing after expenses of no more than $24,000 ($2,000 a month). Imagine, for example, that these owners would agree to sell based on a low cap rate of 8 percent:

$$V = \frac{\$24,000}{.08}$$

$$V = \$300,000$$

If you bought this building for 10 percent down (seller financing) and financed the $270,000 balance over 20 years at an interest rate of 7.5 percent, you would pay the sellers $2,175 a month for a total of $26,098 a year. Not only are these sellers now free to take that trip around the world that they've been dreaming about, they have gained more cash flow from their property.

How the Numbers Work for You   At first glance, you might say, "Wait a minute. I'm the loser in this deal. How can I make any money? Most of my current rent collections will go to the sellers. I'm facing a negative cash flow." You forgot—you're not a passive investor. You're an entrepreneur. You made this investment only because your market analysis showed that the present owners were undermanaging the property. Even without substantial improvements, you know that you can raise rents and boost NOI by 20 percent. After you've brought up the rents to where they should be, the value of your building will climb to $360,000.

$$\$24{,}000 \text{ (old NOI)} \times 1.20 = \$28{,}000 \text{ (new NOI)}$$

$$V \text{ (new value)} = \frac{\$28{,}000}{.08}$$

$$\text{New Value} = \$360{,}000$$

Your before-tax cash flow will now look like this:

$$\text{Gross rents} = \$38{,}400$$

$$\text{Expenses} = 9{,}600$$

$$\text{NOI} = 28{,}800$$

$$\text{Mtg. Pymt.} = 26{,}098$$

$$\text{BTCF} = \$2{,}702$$

$$\text{Cash on cash return} = \frac{\$2{,}702 \text{ (BTCF)}}{\$30{,}000 \text{ (down pymt.)}}$$

$$= 9\%$$

You not only have added $60,000 to the value of the building, your rent increases along with some increases in operating expenses give an immediate cash-on-cash return of 9 percent.

How High Can You Go?

Neither a market study nor the signals of underpricing (wait lists, zero vacancies, complacent tenants) will tell you precisely how far up you can take your rent increases. Your definitive answer will come only by testing the market. Contrary to what you might expect, though, you should test higher and then back down if necessary. If you test lower and immediately succeed, you still don't know the upper limit that you could have achieved.

Test without Risk   You can test high without much risk in several ways:

1. **Test advertise.** Prior to actually getting a vacancy, publicize the specifics of your units in the normal channels (classified ads, housing offices of local colleges, bulletin boards) at the highest rent you could even hope to obtain. If no one calls, you're probably too high. If potential tenants do call, note how many and the intensity of their interest. Six calls the first day—with all callers ready to visit the property—usually indicates you haven't yet hit your top limit.

> **Let tenants tell you your maximum rental rate.**

2. **Test advertise with showing.** Even more informative, when test advertising, follow through with test showings. Make arrangements with one or more of your tenants to permit entry into their unit(s). (Typically, if the tenant has given notice, the lease may—or at least should—give you this right.) During the showing, monitor the prospective resident's comments. Ask pointed questions. Learn all you can about your units and the apartment market as seen through the eyes of actual prospects.

3. **Ask the prospects to bid.** If you actually have a vacancy, schedule a showing with multiple tenants. Then

ask them, "What are you willing to pay?" In hot housing markets, home sellers have used this auction approach to sell their properties for as much as 15 percent or 20 percent over their original asking price.

Use the Call-Back Approach   When you conduct a market survey, you usually compare asking rents. You may see a "for rent" ad or sign, view the unit, and note the price at which the owner (or manager) has placed the property onto the market. To best understand the market, though, follow-up your viewings after a week or two. Telephone the owner and find out whether the unit is still available.

Also, to test the market in various rental categories (unit size, area of town, price range), get a copy of a newspaper that was printed two weeks ago. Go through the classified rental ads. Dial the numbers and discover which units have rented and which ones remain vacant. Use these data to help detect market patterns. You might find emerging strength in the $800 to $1,000 a month two-bedroom market in the northwest area of town, but slowness elsewhere. What does the data signal about how high you might be able to price your units—without incurring prolonged vacancies?

> **Follow up to learn which competitors have found tenants.**

Look closely for those features/locations in strong demand. In cases where your product market looks great, test your rent increases at a higher level. When the market appears to be softening, don't go with the flow. Figure out ways to make your units more desirable. (See Chapter 8.)

Selective Increases

Sometimes a property owner sets a rent schedule for a multi-unit property as follows:

1/1s	$650
2/1s	$785
2/2s	$850

In this type of pricing plan, all units with the same room count are priced at the same rental rate—as if room count alone determined desirability. On closer inspection, though, you might find that some units provide their residents better views, less noise, more convenient parking, or greater privacy. In those instances, you might very well be able to price these units at a premium relative to the others.

> **Room count alone doesn't equal desirability.**

Likewise, depending on your target market, upstairs units may command a higher price than downstairs units, or vice versa. Relative to lower-level units, upstairs apartments typically offer privacy, enhanced security, more natural light, and no noise from above (as in people clomping about). In contrast, some people prefer the first floor because it allows easier access to parking, no stairs to climb, and perhaps lower bills for heating or air conditioning.

Whether upstairs or downstairs, end units tend to deliver more appeal—hence, potentially higher rents. All in all, never price your units solely by room count. Not only do your units compete with other properties, they compete with each other. As you identify those advantages (or disadvantages) within your own building, price accordingly.

Dealing with Current Tenants

Tenants love low rents. But most know when they're getting the proverbial deal "that's too good to last." When a property changes hands, the tenants in the building will expect to see their rents go up. Nevertheless, try to soothe their apprehensions.

Talk with Each Tenant Personally   Ideally, you will have talked with at least several of the tenants prior to buying the building. But now, to the extent possible, meet with each tenant personally. Establish rapport. Ask them what improvements they would like to see occur. Get their feedback. Explain the fact that Mr. and Mrs. Former Owners were actually subsidizing the property operations. They could afford to do so because they had only paid $95,000 for the building 18 years ago. Besides, they no longer even faced mortgage payments.

Will these talks convince all of these tenants that you're a good guy or gal? Will these talks persuade these tenants to gladly pay you an extra $50, $100, or more each month? No. But, at least these efforts will go over much better than a mere written letter that announces a big spike in their rents on the next renewal date for their rental agreement.

> **Provide tenants their *best* deal, not the cheapest deal.**

PVP Revisited Throughout this entire discussion of raising rents, you may think that I have reneged on my principle of PVP—creating a value proposition for tenants that surpasses those offered by other property owners. If so, you've forgotten the second half of that principle, i.e. the value proposition that you provide must also yield you superior profits.

I have not urged you to *arbitrarily* raise rents. Through your study of the market, you have found that rent increases are justified relative to the features and pricing of competitive properties. Even at the higher rent levels, you're still offering as good (or better) a deal than most tenants could find.

In your efforts to appease the current tenants, personal rapport and explanations will go only so far. At the end of the day, tenants will decide to stick with your property primarily because they can't find anything else they like better for the same amount of money. Make sure you also press this all-important point.

Your need for more rental income to cover high mortgage payments, property taxes, and insurance premiums actually count for very little in the minds of your tenants. To retain tenants, first and foremost, make sure they understand the reality of the current market. If they haven't shopped for a place to live for several years, they might face sticker shock. In your one-on-one talks, bring these tenants up to date on rental rates. (You might also remind them of the dollar costs and personal hassle that moving to a new residence creates.)

Can You Boost Your Rent Collections by Lowering Rents?

For the past six months, I have kept my eye on a rental house that I pass frequently. The house shows well, it's conveniently located in a professional neighborhood of single-family, predominantly owner-occupied houses within a 10-minute bike ride of a major university and the city's central business district (CBD). Yet for all of these past six months, the house has sat vacant. Why?

Because the owners started out by asking a rent of $1,500 per month. After four months with no takers, they dropped their price to $1,250, which is still the *asking rent* today. The true *market rent* range for this house tops at $1,000.

An Extreme Example of Overpricing and Market Ignorance (or Fanciful Dreaming)

Although a wildly extreme example of fanciful pricing in a weak upscale market, that is, an upscale rental for this town, it does illustrate the point. Sometimes you can actually boost your rent collections and profits by lowering rents. Because rent levels, tenant turnover, and vacancy losses tend to move up (or down) together, you must continually monitor the market to find those trade-off levels that maximize profits. If one or more of your units sit vacant for two or three weeks, you're probably over market. If you watch a unit sit vacant for six months, people will begin to question your sanity.

> **Lower rents can boost profits.**

A Purchase Opportunity

Sometimes an owner of a rental property gets into deep water without a life vest. He buys a property, underestimates its expenses, and tries to salvage his cash flows by increasing rents. Of course, these rent increases (absent a market justification) make matters worse. Vacancies climb to 20 percent. Rent collections fall. More tenants give notice that they won't be renewing their leases. Turnovers mount. The distressed owner misses several mortgage payments and begins to feel the heat of the lender's lawyers.

Although this situation spells trouble for the distressed owner, it spells opportunity for the entrepreneurial investor who can solve the problem: To get rent collections up, reduce rents.

It's far better to achieve 95 percent occupancy with a rental rate of $800 a month than struggle with 80 percent occupancy at a rent level of $850. Consider the figures for this 24-unit building:

Above Market Rents (80 Percent Occupancy)

1.   24 (units) $\times$ $850 $\times$ 12 $\times$ .80 = $195,840

Top of Market Rents (95 Percent Occupancy)

2.   24 units $\times$ $800 $\times$ 12 $\times$ .95 = $218,880

> **Owners who maximize occupancy don't necessarily maximize profits.**

As you can see, the rent collections at the lower rent of $800 per month actually yield more cash. But look what happens if we charge rents of $725 a month to try to achieve (or sustain) that mythical ideal of zero vacancies (100 percent occupancy):

Below Market Rents (100 Percent Occupancy)

3.   24 (units) $\times$ $725 $\times$ 12 $\times$ 1.0 = $208,000

Naturally, the precise break points in rents, vacancies, and rent collections will vary over time by area, price range, and building features. Yet, the basic principle holds in all places at all times:

Continually monitor the market. Never cease your search to determine those rental rates that will maximize the net income of the property if your goal is to maximize the value of the property.

Time-Sensitive Rental Markets

In some locations, you can achieve peak rents only if you get your properties rented within a window of opportunity. In most college towns, vacancies in August typically rent faster and at higher rents than in, say, November or June. In Sarasota, Florida (and other winter vacation spots), December may prove to perform best. In April, the snowbirds have left and vacancies proliferate. In the Hamptons, the summer brings top rents. But you better have your leases signed by Spring because in May and June, owners start to become desperate and slash their asking rents.

In contrast to typical rental seasons, on occasion, in extremely tight markets, you can extract premium rents after the period of peak activity ends. In those cases, because virtually all properties now have tenants, those rare vacancies that do occur may be able to take advantage of their scarcity—providing that the market still includes many renters looking for a place to land—even after the music has stopped.

> **Learn the rental season of your local market.**

The moral: Know the timing of the markets where you own properties. Some areas cycle through peaks and valleys every year. If you see your window of opportunity closing, it's usually better to cut rents sooner rather than later.

Build Equity Fast with Sharp Interiors

You can build equity fast when you recognize how to collect more rents from an existing property. But to really accelerate your wealth building, you need to create value for your properties and your residents through various improvements and changes. Frequently, you can bring in more rents, cut expenses, and lower a building's cap rate—all at the same time. By simultaneously achieving all of these goals, you can jump the value of a property by 30 to 40 percent within a period as short as 24 months. But you're probably going to work for this reward.

The Entrepreneurial Imperative

As I have mentioned, with continuing stock market turmoil and uncertainty, hundreds of thousands of investors have decided to shift their asset allocation away from stocks and toward real estate. Given the extraordinarily exaggerated hopes and fantasies that 50 million investors recently held for stocks, I believe this rush to real estate will continue. But let me recap the problem.

Too Many Investors

Too many investors are chasing (and will continue to chase) too few good properties. For the past several months I have been aggressively searching for small income properties, primarily in Florida, but also in other areas of the country. The only "instant" equity deals (that is, value creation through quick rent increases) that I'm finding are in low- to moderate-income properties. Although I have previously earned huge returns in the low-moderate market, these properties no longer fit my objectives. (Nevertheless, I still believe that these properties make a great starting point for beginning investors because they yield high cash flows and often sell at affordable prices.)

> **The low hanging fruit gets picked quickly.**

Notwithstanding the low-moderate market, to get that juicy 30 percent boost in value in today's market will typically require entrepreneurial talents. To score big, you must blend together market savvy, creativity, and a true desire to deliver a better product to your target market. You must see what others don't see. You must perform at a level that most people won't perform.

Too Few Sellers

Recently I saw the following ad:

> West side of Bradenton: Duplex, Triplex, 8-plex or 29 units. 6.4 GRM, positive cash flow—20% down. Bronson Realty—(987) 654-3210.

I called the first day and left a message that I wanted to see the properties. No response. In follow-up about two weeks later, I talked with the listing broker. He told me that he had received 60 calls on the property and apologized for not getting back to me. But then, even worse news. The seller had withdrawn the properties from the market in favor of refinancing. "Why should he sell and pay taxes when a cash-out refinance will put just as much money in the investor's pocket?" the broker asked rhetorically when relaying the investor's reasons for deciding not to sell. Unfortunately for new investors, low interest rates are making property ownership much more profitable for existing investors. Lower interest rates mean lower mortgage payments and higher cash flows. Besides, "if I sell" investors say to themselves, "where will I be able to reinvest the money that beats the returns I'm now earning with these income properties?"

Not Words of Discouragement

Don't misinterpret me. I'm not trying to discourage you. Quite the opposite. I want to encourage you to get started now so that in 5, 10, or 15 years (depending on your goals and commitment), you will sit comfortably in a financial position similar to today's owners who bought 5, 10, or 15 years ago.

> **Today's "high" prices will seem low as you look back in 2013.**

When you look at properties today, don't focus on the past opportunities that you missed. Don't focus on the seller's "ridiculously" low cap rate and "absurdly" high asking price. Instead, focus on the value that you can create for that property. Think how much equity you're going to build in that property as you figure out ways to lift its NOI. If your careful analysis doesn't reveal potential for the property, move on to the next seller.

Even in tight markets, some owners hit financial hard times. They get divorced, suffer management burnout, become complacent, or see other ventures they want to pursue. When you look, you will always find motivated sellers with opportunity-laden properties. Even better, after you become known in your local market, the deals will come to you. After I had been buying properties for only two or three years, the sellers from which I had bought began recommending me to their landlording friends who now wanted to sell. Often, these referrals brought easy deals without the friction of a real estate commission.

Your Target Market

> **Select the qualified tenant who most wants the unit.**

Nearly every book on property management tells you to thoroughly screen your tenants; then select the applicant(s) who are *most* qualified. I differ with this advice. I believe you should select the most appreciative tenant who is qualified. The most appreciative tenant is the one who most highly values what you're offering, and is willing and able to pay the highest rents.

Visualize Your Tenants

Perhaps owners who offer a generic property to a generic tenant can select customers by their credit scores and references. But entrepreneurs go further. To whom do you want to appeal?

- Families with small children
- College students
- Seniors
- Nurses who work at the nearby hospital
- Young professional singles who live as roommates
- Workers at the local factory
- Who else?

Or you might think in terms of certain amenities such as quiet, natural light, spaciousness, storage, or convenience. Remember, when you study the market (competing properties along with the dislikes, preferences, needs, and wants of various types of tenants), you're not really attempting to discover "market" rent levels per se. You're attempting to discover features/attributes in high demand by certain people, but rarely found. Consider that property owners tend to fall into four categories:

◆ Never do anything more than is absolutely necessary.
◆ Maintain the property enough to preserve its condition.
◆ Cosmetically enhance the property according to the owner's tastes.
◆ Entrepreneurially enhance the property.

Why do entrepreneurs outperform these other types of property owners? Because they visualize their future tenants. We can say that entrepreneurs try to get inside their customers' minds. They persistently ask, "How would my preferred tenant react to . . . ? Would they react with an excited 'Wow,' a bland 'It's okay,' or a repulsive 'Ugh. . . .' "

Your Suggestion Box

In the following pages, you will read dozens of ideas. Weigh and consider these ideas as you would those you might pull out of a suggestion box. Some you can use immediately. Some you can't. But don't throw any of them away.

Each time you evaluate a property as a potential investment, run through these ideas again. Ask yourself, "For the types of tenants that I have in mind, would this change bolster the value proposition that I could offer? Will this change create a competitive advantage for this property which will bolster my bottom line?" When you look at properties with an entrepreneurial eye, you will see profit potential that escapes the notice of most sellers, and most other investors. In today's market (and most certainly in tomorrow's market), that's how you will find most of your deals.

> **Learn to envision what others fail to see.**

Figuring Payback

When you find a property that warrants improvement, you figure your payback with a variant of the value formula that we've been using . . .

$$V = \frac{NOI}{R}$$

Only in this instance, the V refers to value created and the NOI refers to the additional net income that your apartments will bring in after you have performed your magic. Say your improvements add $100 a month per unit to NOI. If the applicable cap rate is 10 percent, through your work, you've created $12,000 in added value for that unit.

$$V = \frac{\$1,200 \ (12 \ \times \ \$100/unit}{.10}$$

$$V = \$12,000$$

How much should you be willing to invest to achieve that $12,000 per unit increase in value? Personally, I figure a 2:1 ratio. For each $1 in value created, I prefer not to invest any more than 50¢. But technically, you could invest up to 99.9¢ (or a total of $11,999 in this instance) and you would still net a profit.

Fast Buck versus the Last Buck

Generally, most entrepreneurs go for the fast buck, not the last buck. In other words, through your improvements, don't try to improve everything. Instead, through your study of the market, identify those changes that create the most revenue for the least amount of outlay and the lowest risk. Your tenants operate on a budget, and so must you. The closer you push your rents toward the top end of the neighborhood (or the top end of your tenants' willingness and ability to pay), the more you risk overshooting your target.

Setting Your Budget for Improvements

To decide how much money to allocate to changes within a property, imagine that after your review of the property and the market, you develop the following list of possibilities:

Improvement	Cost	Added Rent/Mo.
Thorough cleaning	$ 400	$ 75
Paint and carpet	2,000	50
Kitchen bath redo	5,000	100
Ceiling fans	250	5
New windows	3,000	35
Fireplace	2,500	25
Kitchen appliances	1,250	25
Covered parking	1,500	15
Balcony/deck	2,500	10
New HVAC (energy efficient)	2,000	20
Total	$20,400	$360

Theoretically, all of these improvements would cost a total of $20,400 and would boost your rents by $360 a month. Using the widely accepted formula, you can see that these improvements will add about $43,200 to the value of each unit.

$$V = \frac{4{,}320 \ (12 \times \$360)}{.10}$$

$$V = \$43{,}200$$

Is this number reasonable? Not likely. Unless you're dealing with high dollar rentals in an expensive area, you've raised your rents too high. You need to go back and choose those improvements that will give you the highest return that your tenants are willing to pay. You might wean your possibilities as follows:

Improvement	Cost	Added Rent/Mo.
Cleaning	$ 400	$ 75
Paint and carpet	2,000	50
Kitchen bath redo	5,000	100
Appliances	1,250	25
Total	$8,650	$250

Placing these numbers in the value equation, you get

$$V = \frac{3,000 \ (12 \times \$250)}{.10}$$

$$V = 30,000$$

Even if you boosted rents by only $200 per month, your value created would still give you a payback of about 3:1.

The Sum Effect

In deciding what improvements to make, you would typically try to imagine the sum effect of your changes on the tenant's willingness to rent the property. Sometimes you include some low payback items (on an individual basis) for the synergistic or "nice touch" effect that they will add to the total project.

> **Aim your improvements toward an overall effect.**

Naturally, in working through the previous numbers, you will never be able to precisely calculate cost and return. But, if you rely on this methodology, it will force you to think through your possibilities. Yet at the same time, avoid overdoing the project. Use this method to maximize your opportunity to get the most bang for the buck.

The Interior of the Units

Most investors breeze through a property and then size it up by saying something like this, "Well, these units should go for maybe $550 a month, $575 tops. Let me run the numbers and see how they come out." In contrast, to lay the foundation for creating value, you would not dwell exclusively on the monetary value of the rental unit; rather, you would closely examine it as would someone (from your target market) who is considering this apartment for their home. In fact, try to pre-inspect the apartment even more closely than many residents would. Units that eventually disappoint their residents lead to complaints and turnover.

> **Imagine yourself living in the unit. What changes would you want?**

Sharpen the Aesthetics

As you walk into the unit, are you met with a bland neutrality? Do you see faded paint, scuff marks, outdated color schemes, cheap hollow-core doors, nail holes in the walls, worn carpeting, torn linoleum, old-fashioned light fixtures, cracked wall switch plates, or stained sinks? If you answer yes to any or all of these questions, great! You've found the easiest path to creating value.

Pay Special Attention to Kitchens and Baths   To really wow your potential tenants, bring in Martha Stewart to redo the kitchens and bathrooms. Flip through the pages of those many kitchen and bath magazines. Look for that right combination of materials and colors that will create a light, bright, cheerful, and inviting look. Eliminate those harvest gold appliances, the chipped and stained sinks, and that cracked glass in the shower door.

As you inspect the kitchen and baths, focus for at least 30 seconds on each of the following:

◆ Floors
◆ Ceilings
◆ Sinks
◆ Toilet bowl
◆ Windows and window sills
◆ Electrical outlet plates
◆ Lighting

◆ Faucets
◆ Walls
◆ Cabinets
◆ Cabinet and drawer handles
◆ Appliances
◆ Counter tops

By focusing for 30 seconds on each ingredient in these rooms, you will notice everything that blends together to give these rooms their overall flavor. Throughout the entire apartment, details count. But they especially count in the kitchens and bathrooms. The right pizzazz in the kitchens and bathrooms can transform a ho-hum unit into a showplace.

How much will this transformation cost? If you've recently spent $25,000 to remodel your own kitchen, you may think pizzazz in a rental unit would break the bank. Not true. You can accomplish showcase makeovers with an outlay of between $2,000 and $5,000. Replacing sinks, cabinetry hardware, toilet bowls, and toilet seats requires relatively little money. As to cabinetry, most often a refinish (not a full replacement) can achieve your goals.

Cleanliness Generates Profits   Do you want to attract tenants who will care for your properties? Then thoroughly clean the units as if a drill sergeant were about to perform a white glove inspection. Do not think, "rental property." Think, "home."

Clean everywhere. Remove the dirt, dust, cob webs, and dead bugs from all corners, baseboards, light fixtures, and shelving. Pull out all kitchen drawers. Dump the bread crumbs and other accumulated debris. Wipe them clean. Make sure all windows and mirrors sparkle and shine. Look closely for grime in the shower and shower door tracks. Scrape the rust out of the medicine cabinets and repaint where necessary. Eliminate all foul odors. The apartment should not only look fresh and clean, it should smell fresh and clean.

Some owners of small income properties clean their units superficially. They figure, "It's only a rental. Why go to all of that trou-

> **Cleanliness pays back at least tenfold.**

ble and expense?" In fact, though, cleanliness pays back more than any other improvement. It's the easiest way for you to give your properties a competitive edge. More importantly, the best tenants will pay for cleanliness. You achieve two goals simultaneously: more money from better tenants.

Natural Light and Views   If your units seem dark, brighten them up. In addition to color schemes, consider adding windows or skylights. If you're lucky, you might find one of those older buildings with 10' ceilings—now reduced to 8' via suspended acoustical tile. For a reason unknown to me (energy conservation?), dropped ceilings became widely popular in the 1970s. Today, they're considered ugly and outdated. Rip out those dropped ceilings. Your rooms will seem larger and brighter. Also, in rooms with high ceilings, install clerestory windows to bring in more light.

For first-floor units, see if you can enhance the view with landscaping or fencing. For upper-story units, think long term. Plant trees. Although seldom financially feasible, you might create a view by moving a window. Ugly views turn off most tenants. Pleasant views provide good selling points. Do as much as you can to ameliorate (or eliminate) the former and enhance the latter.

Special Touches

For those special aesthetic touches, try chair railings, wallpaper borders, upgraded door handles, paneled doors, and wood stains (rather than paint). Upgrades in light fixtures, too, can help you add pizzazz. Newer forms of track lighting seem to be gaining popularity in some areas for both form and function.

You can get ideas for special touches not only from the many types of home decorating and remodeling magazines, but also by visiting new model homes and newer upscale apartment, townhouse, and condominium developments. You can't go too far with

Add special touches that impress.	special touches or you will cut into your profitability. Nevertheless, a few "gee whiz" features will help rental prospects to favorably differentiate and remember your units vis-à-vis the other properties they've inspected.

Safety, Security, and Functionality

Often safety and functionality go together as with the number and capacity of electrical outlets. Older buildings, especially, lack enough outlets and amperage to safely handle all of the modern household's plug-in appliances, computers, printers, fax machines, and audio/video (a.k.a. home entertainment centers). Many renters don't notice this type of functional obsolescence until after they move into a unit. Then they "solve" the problem with adapter plugs and roaming extension cords. If the apartment lacks electrical capacity, plan an upgrade.

Other Issues of Safety and Security   Other types of safety issues pertain to smoke alarms, carbon monoxide detectors, fire escape routes, door locks, first-floor windows, and first-floor sliding glass doors. Environmental health hazards may exist because of lead paint, asbestos, or formaldehyde—any of which may be found in building materials used in construction (or remodeling) prior to 1978. Insist on written seller disclosures about the presence of any of these hazards. If the building is suspect, don't buy it without securing the advice of an environmental expert.

Don't gloss over potential environmental problems. Get expert help.

Seldom will environmental improvements pay back with higher rents. To profitably deal with environmental issues, you must secure a large discount in price at the time of purchase. As to security against break-ins, make sure all windows and doors lock securely and cannot be jimmied with a credit card (as in the TV shows), or even a screwdriver. Dead bolt locks are best. Entry door peepholes also provide a sense of security.

In our criminal-infested world, tenants want to feel safe in their homes. If doors, door locks, and windows seem flimsy, many tenants won't rent the unit—regardless of its other positive features.

Stairs, Carpets, and Bathrooms   Pay particular attention to any steps or stair railings that may be loose or dangerous. Frayed carpets and bathtubs without no-slip bottoms and handrails can also provoke falls. All in all, you should remedy every safety or security hazard within the property. Even when a repair or modification doesn't lift your rent collections, it will protect your tenants and reduce the chance that you could end up responsible for a tenant's loss.

Rightsizing Room Count/Room Size

Robert Griswald (*Property Management for Dummies,* Wiley, 2000) tells of buying a 12-unit building composed of all two-bedroom, one-bath apartments. Because the building was located just one-and-a-half miles from a college campus, he originally thought he would attract two students (roommates) to the units. But to his surprise, that strategy failed.

> "Although many prospective tenants looked at the units," Griswald reports, "our leasing went very slow and our vacancies remained unacceptable. Clearly, I was trying to define and force the rental market and prospective renters to adapt to my perception of their needs. [When it dawned on me that I would have to change my plan] I began to carefully review the comments of prospective tenants and actually listen to their needs. I found that there was a strong market for faculty and graduate students but they preferred to live alone."

> **Listen carefully to tenant feedback.**

Griswald then further discovered that faculty and graduate students primarily wanted quiet and a place to work or study without noise or interruptions from roommates. With this more accurate picture of needs, he says, "I quickly realized that I could market these very same two-bedroom, one-bath units to this new target market. . . . [So] I revised my marketing effort and changed my ads in the college newspaper to read,

'1-Bedroom plus den.'"

With that change in advertised room count, Griswald says that he was still able to reach his originally intended market, but only after "changing" the product to better fit what that market wanted. Griswald then provides advice that matches perfectly my theme in this book:

"Remember: Look at your rental property from the perspective of the most likely tenants. Then promote and accentuate the features of your rental property that will prove of greatest interest to that market."

Rightsizing the Easy Way   Fortunately for Griswald, in this instance he was able to rightsize the room count (two-bedroom/one-bath → one-bedroom/one-den/one-bath) without making any serious changes to the physical property. Great idea! But you can also rightsize the room count by removing walls, combining units, or subdividing units. At one time in Manhattan, four-bedroom apartments generated very strong demand against short supply, whereas two-bedroom apartments experienced slow demand against a glut of vacancies. In recognizing this market imbalance, an entrepreneurial investor bought a building of two-bedroom apartments at a steeply depressed purchase price and then combined the two-bedroom units into the much sought-

> **Always search for the most profitable room count.**

after four-bedroom apartments. He next quickly rented the new larger units at premium prices.

Downsizing Can Also Work   As a rule, the profit potential from rightsizing the room count tends to favor downsizing over upsizing. That's because smaller units typically rent for a higher price per room than larger units. Consider the following rent schedule:

Unit Type	Monthly Rent
Efficiency	$ 950
1-bedroom/1-bath	$1,100
2-bedroom/2-bath	$1,350

In a rental market where this type of rent gradient exists, you might rightsize a building by converting some of those two-bedroom/ two-bath units into efficiencies. If in this situation, you could cut each two-bedroom apartment into two efficiencies, your rent collections for that space would jump from $1,350 per month to $1,900 per month. Of course, you would need to factor in the conversion costs to determine whether your payback would make you enough money. But the principle holds: At times, market imbalances can create profit opportunities by rightsizing the room counts of the units.

Rightsize the Room Sizes   Have you ever walked into a house and found some rooms too large and others too small? It seems today that in many houses builders construct a huge great room along with a huge master bedroom and bath, and then round off the house with three or four dink-sized bedrooms. The house lacks a sense of proportion, which evidently is what some home-buyers like.

What "sense of proportion" should an apartment display? The answer varies by tenant segment, price range, and timing (that is, tastes today differ from those of 10, 20, or 30 years ago). Thus, as market supply and demand changes, opportunities arise for entrepreneurs to notice room size imbalances. Buy an out-of-style building; then rearrange the internal space in the units to command more appeal to today's intended market segment.

Create More Storage

Do you know that self-storage (mini-warehouses) now represents one of the fastest growing types of properties in the United States? We've all become pack rats. "Throw it away? Why I might need that sometime."

> **Nearly all tenants will pay for more storage space.**

Talk with tenants. Talk with homeowners. Many will tell you the same thing. "I like my home, but we lack enough space for storage." If you want to add appeal to your units, add storage space. To do so, you can think about storage in three ways:

- Bring dead space to life
- Increase the efficiency of existing space
- Create new storage space external to the apartment units

Bring Dead Space to Life   Let me illustrate with what seems trivial, but in fact always creates a lasting favorable impression. Look in the cabinet under your kitchen sink. You will see a small gap between the front panel of the cabinet above the door and the sink. In other words, dead space. How might you use that space? Install a small pull-down compartment to stow soap, sponge, and Brillo pads. No more sink clutter. Whenever I show this little innovation to other people, I always get a "Wow, isn't that neat," type of response.

Okay, I admitted it's trivial. But it illustrates the point. All homes and apartments include generous amounts of large and small dead spaces that with creativity you can bring to life:

- Under stairs and stairwells
- Bay windows with storage built under the window seat and under the outside of the window

- ◆ Garden windows
- ◆ On the tops of kitchen cabinets
- ◆ Dead-end cabinets
- ◆ Walls suitable for shelving
- ◆ Recessed storage between studs (as with an in-wall medicine chest)
- ◆ Kitchen hanging bars for pots and pans

These ideas represent just a sampling of possibilities. If you carefully inspect any home or apartment and then ask, "Where are the dead spaces that I can bring to life for purposes of storage?" I guarantee that you will find them.

Rightsize Existing Storage Space   My favorite examples to illustrate this point come from the California Closet Company (CCC). As this innovative firm has proven, you can double (or triple) your storage capacity without adding even one square inch of new space. Simply reorganize and redesign the raw space that already exists. Although founded as a closet company, CCC now redesigns garages, offices, workshops, and kitchens. Put these same organizing principles to work and you'll truly enhance the appeal of your rental properties.

> **Make existing space work more effectively.**

You could also multi-purpose some space. The most common way to achieve this end is through use of a Murphy bed that folds up into a wall. This not only increases usable floor area, but also you can install shelving alongside the bed. You can either use the wall cavity or create a new, larger cavity by bringing a new wall out even with the Murphy bed.

Create New Space External to the Unit   Why let your tenant dollars flow to a self-storage company? Create more storage right on your property that will bring in additional revenue. (We will discuss this topic along with other ideas to generate more income from your properties in Chapter 9.)

Check Noise Levels

Noise is a potential problem within apartments. Will sound from a television or stereo carry into other rooms? Bring along a portable radio on your building inspections. Place it in various rooms. Turn up the volume. Do the walls provide enough soundproofing? Families and roommate tenants want privacy and quiet. If your property fails to offer these essentials, your property will lose its appeal.

Just as important, will your tenants hear neighbors or neighborhood noise from inside their units? Again, people pay for quiet. They discount heavily for noise.

Although potential neighbors and neighborhood noise are especially important to consider in areas filled with multi-family housing, as noted earlier, predominantly single-family areas may also feature loud stereos, barking dogs, and Indy 500 engine revving. Does the drum corps of the nearby high school practice outside three or four hours a day? When possible, visit the property during periods of high traffic or peak noise. Don't assume that a peaceful looking neighborhood actually offers peace and quiet. Verify before you buy.

Seek written disclosures from the seller of the property. Talk with neighbors. Determine whether anyone has tried to enforce quiet by complaining to city government, a homeowners association, or by filing a nuisance suit? If you buy the property, could you effectively invoke any of these remedies against tenants (or homeowners) in other nearby properties? Could your building itself incorporate more features to reduce noise that emanates from either the outside or the inside of the building? When you suppress noise into quiet, you create value.

Overall Livability of the Unit

Once again, remember that you are not running a "rental property." You are providing people with a home. In your summary analysis

> **Create a home, not merely a rental unit.**

of the units weigh the overall livability of the units for your intended market of residents.

◆ Do the units offer enough square footage?
◆ Are the units spotlessly clean, fresh, and bright? Do they smell clean and fresh?
◆ Does the room count represent the most profitable configuration of space?
◆ Do the aesthetics of the units excite with emotional appeal?
◆ Does the unit bring in enough natural light?
◆ What views will the tenants see from inside the units looking out?
◆ Do the units offer generous amounts of closets and storage space?
◆ Are the units quiet?
◆ Does the floor plan make for efficient traffic flow?
◆ Will tenants feel safe and secure within the units?
◆ Do the kitchens and baths offer a competitive pizzazz?

When you improve the units to transform a rental property into a home, you will achieve high rents and low vacancies.

Generate More Income

Great livable units that sparkle with pizzazz and emotional appeal will keep your building full of tenants who will gladly pay premium prices. But before sharp interiors can woo your prospective tenants, you must get them to keep their appointments to inspect the "homes" you are offering. Nothing will accomplish this goal any better than curb appeal.

You can write an award-winning newspaper ad that will make your phone ring. Yet, this literary prowess will fall flat when great tenants pull up in front of the building and immediately begin to ask themselves, "What are we doing here? This place is nothing like I imagined. Do you think we should go in?"

"Nah, why waste our time? This place is a dump. We shouldn't even think about living here."

Your Building Is Your Best Advertisement

More than likely, hundreds (or even thousands) of people will pass by your property each week. What, if anything, will they notice about it? Will it appear as that rundown "rental" of the neighborhood, a nondescript plain Jane, or it just might elicit this response,

> **Advertise your property with a well-kept outstanding exterior.**

"Isn't that building kept up well? Those flower gardens and brick walkways seem to reach out and invite people to come inside."

If you want your building to generate more income, create an inviting exterior. Create award-winning publicity with knock-out curb appeal. Not only will an attractive, well-kept exterior appeal to a better class of tenants, it will also increase tenant satisfaction and reduce turnover.

Clean Up the Grounds

When you first take over a property, carry out a detailed clean-up of the grounds, parking area, and walkways. Pick up trash, accumulated leaves, fallen tree branches. Erect a fence to block the view of the dumpsters or other trash disposal areas. To the extent the current leases or municipal law permits, get tenants to remove any inoperable cars from the parking lots, parking spaces, or driveways. If such cars are parked on the streets, ask the city government to post them and tow them.

Porches, patios, decks, and yards should remain free of useless household items such as discarded furniture, appliances, car parts, motorcycles, bicycles, kid's toys, and all other items that give the property a dilapidated, uncared-for look. Step one toward curb appeal requires a super neat and debris-free appearance.

Yard Care and Landscaping

Here's where you can really add value to a property. Tenants and homebuyers alike love a manicured lawn, flower-lined walkways, mulched shrubs, and flower gardens. With landscaping, you can turn an ugly duckling building into a showcase property. With landscaping you can create privacy, manufacture a gorgeous view looking out from the inside of the units, or eliminate an ugly view.

Especially if you're looking at a three to five year holding period (or longer), put in those small plants, shrubs, flower gardens, and hedges now. When you sell, you can easily earn a return of at least 10:1.

> **Over time, landscaping provides huge returns. Start now.**

Of course, you want to plant only low-maintenance grass and vegetation. You don't want to pay a yard maintenance company a small fortune. Maybe one of your tenants might even enjoy yard artistry and you could cut a deal. For lawn and landscape ideas that will work best in your geographic area of the country, talk with several landscape companies. Avoid buying plants just because some nursery has put them on sale and you can load up your SUV for a pittance. Take time to learn what plants will grow best with the least work and lowest chance of disease and early death.

And don't forget to look for good places to plant trees. Over the mid- to longer term, well-located trees will give you a very favorable payback. Learn their height and width at maturity. Many amateurs plant young trees and shrubs too close to the building.

Sidewalks, Walkways, and Parking Areas

Replace or repair major cracks and buckling that may appear in your sidewalks and parking areas. Remove all grass or weeds that may be growing through the cracks. Edge all of the areas where the yard abuts concrete or asphalt. Neatness pays. Overgrown grass and weeds really stain the curb appeal of a rental property—precisely because these types of blemishes signal that the property is a rental.

Also remove oil stains from parking areas. If parking for the property proves inadequate to the number of cars the tenants own, create more parking area. Don't allow tenants (or anyone else) to park in the yard. Mark all parking areas, and restrict all parking to those designated areas.

Fences, Lampposts, and Mailboxes

For purposes of aesthetics, privacy, and security, quality fencing can enhance the value of a property. Just as certainly, a rusted, rotted, or half-falling down fence clearly blemishes the property. Likewise for rusty lampposts with broken glass light fixtures.

For a nice decorative touch, add a white picket fence or a low-level stone fence in the front of the building. If the building houses a

> **Clean up the mailbox area and keep it clean.**

cluster of mailboxes, make sure the mail area is kept neat and the mailboxes present a good first impression. Too many careless property owners allow the mail areas to accumulate with junk mail, advertising circulars, unwanted magazines, and other items from the post office that are addressed to persons who no longer live in the building. If each unit has its own mailbox, replace them with attractive new ones. Sharpen the unit numbers, too.

The Exterior of the Building

Along with thoroughly improving the site, turn your attention to the exterior of the building(s). The building must signal to prospective tenants that this owner takes good care of his property. To evaluate the building's exterior and generate ideas for improvements, focus on these four criteria:

- ◆ Appearance
- ◆ Condition
- ◆ Building materials and maintenance expense
- ◆ Site placement (how the building is oriented on the site)

Appearance As you begin to inspect the building exterior, stand back at least 50 to 100 feet. Place the building in perspective with the site and with other properties in the neighborhood. Does it fit in? Does the architectural style give the

> **Stand back from the property. Evaluate each detail that contributes to (or detracts from) the exterior.**

property an appealing uniqueness, or is it a simple rectangular box design with no windows on either side? Have a half dozen other apartment buildings in the neighborhood been built with the same bland design? What improvements can you make to the building that will enhance its appearance and favorably set it off from nearby properties as well as other competitive buildings?

◆ **The roof.** Pay special attention to the roof. Is it discolored? Are leaves piling up? Are plants growing on the roof or out of the rusty gutters? A roof can dramatically influence the exterior aesthetics of a building because it frequently occupies 30 percent or more of what you see when you face a building. Clean it up so that it shows as little wear as possible.

If your remedial efforts can't improve the appearance of the roof—and you're planning to quickly flip the property—consider replacing it. As the real estate expert Bob Bruss points out, a new roof probably won't give you a dollar-for-dollar payback, but it will enhance the property's marketability. On occasion, such "loss leader" repairs can work synergistically to create an overall effect that will help your property rent or sell for a higher amount.

◆ **Cosmetic makeover.** Can you imagine ways to enhance the building's appearance with shutters, flower boxes, dramatic front door(s) and entryways, new or additional windows, fresh paint, a contrasting color for trim, or accenting the design with architectural details? How well does (or could) the property's exterior distinguish it from other comparably-priced rental properties? Do you rate its appeal as great, so-so, or awful? List other possibilities for profitable improvements.

Think of features that will really set your property apart from its competitors. Look for those features that will wow your target market and passersby.

Exterior Condition: The Professional Inspection   To avoid too many loss leader repairs, you will hire a professional home inspector to detect potential problems with any property you offer to buy.

> **Use your inspection to negotiate a lower price.**

Generally, though, you won't order an inspection report until after you've signed a purchase contract that includes an inspection contingency clause. Nevertheless, prior to that step, perform a close pre-professional inspection. Your personal scrutiny of the exterior (and interior) will serve three purposes.

1. **Purchase negotiations.** To achieve the best price and terms, you must justify your offer. When the seller says, "What! You're offering me $415,000! Buildings like this are selling for $60,000 a unit." "Yes," you respond. "But those buildings are in near perfect condition. As we discussed, this property is going to need. . . ."
2. **Weed out losers.** When your pre-inspection clearly identifies problems yet the seller won't accommodate you with concessions, stop wasting time. Say sayonara. Move on to your next possibility.
3. **Education and understanding.** When you do bring a professional inspector in, don't settle for a mere inspection. Go for an education. Use your pre-inspection notes to quiz the pro. Learn all you can about spotting problems, and understand their cause, remedial alternatives, and most importantly, cost effective means of prevention.

Materials and Maintenance   Each area of the country has its own types of construction materials that are popular and effective for that locale. Wood, brick, brick veneer, adobe, concrete block, stucco, and steel are possibilities. In addition, some buildings are built on a pier-and-beam foundation; others sit on concrete slabs. Windows and roofs differ, too. Crank-style aluminum awning windows are popular in some warmer climates but seldom found up north. In California, you see tile roofs; in Maine, that type of roof is rare.

Evaluate the quality of construction and building materials. Regardless of the specific types of construction materials used in your area, you can bet that they vary widely in costs, function, and desirability. Before buying, talk to knowledgeable builders, contractors, or building supply companies to learn the differences between high-end, mid-range, and low-cost building materials. Maybe you can talk with someone who has recently built a new house. They may have spent months shopping for and comparing materials. Unlike your tenants, you've got to move beyond appearance. Savvy investors don't judge the quality of a building by its paint job.

Maintenance: Time, effort, and costs. Apart from the quality of construction materials, consider how much time, effort, and money it's going to cost to maintain the building. Growing up, I recall that every three or four years we had to scrape peeling paint with a wire brush to prepare our home for its next coat of paint. Now, today's durable paints, stains, and materials often last 10 years or longer.

> **Favor low maintenance buildings.**

When you do repair or renovate, go with low- or no-maintenance improvements, even if they cost more. You, your eventual buyers, or your tenants don't want to fool around with property maintenance. Low- or no-maintenance features will boost your property's net income and help it retain its pleasing appearance for a longer period of time.

For lower- to moderate-priced properties, I strongly favor vinyl siding and eaves. In the South, I like concrete block. Slap on a coat of paint every 15 to 20 years and that's it for exterior maintenance. As to gutters, old-timers love them. I hate them. The best way to deal with rusty, leaf-filled gutters—rip them off and don't replace them. Place a rain diverter on the roof above the exterior entryways.

As I have said before, I possess no talent, no inclination, and no time to personally take on the chores of property repair and property maintenance. With today's materials, that distaste erects no barriers to owning rental properties.

Building Placement　In looking at a building from the outside, note how it is situated on the site. Are the windows positioned to bring in beacons of natural light? How about privacy from neighbors? Can residents sunbathe in the backyard without prying eyes invading their privacy? Are the sleeping areas of the units protected from street noise? How will prevailing winter winds (or summer breezes) strike the building? How will these affect resident comfort and energy bills? In North America, a southern exposure with large windows will bring in the winter sunshine and reduce heating costs.

> **Tenants love units with loads of natural light.**

Safety and security.　Notice whether you spot any safety or security hazards. Is the building situated such that residents can enter publicly viewed areas? I once owned a building where entrances to two of the units required residents to walk down a long narrow passageway with a tall fence on one side and a hedge row. Although I never thought about it back then, today I would make sure that passageway was very well-lighted at night.

Not only might someone fall in the dark, but the dark walkway could prove attractive to a mugger or rapist. Today, you must always try to reasonably provide for the safety and security of your tenants whether they're inside their units or simply walking up to an entryway from the street or a designated parking area.

Topography.　I once owned a property that was sited slightly below grade. After every hard rain, water flowed into the garage as if it were transported there by an aqueduct. In addition to drainage, topography will affect the slope of the entrance way to the property. Even moderate inclines can make navigation up or down difficult during snow and ice storms. Topography also can increase renovation costs and expose a site to greater risk from mudslide or earthquake.

Note, too, egress and ingress. Apart from navigating a driveway during ice and snow, does the property's site produce any other problems for residents as they pull in and out of the property? Traffic? Does the building itself block a view of whether cars are oncoming. Even relatively slight difficulties of egress and ingress can deter people from renting units in a building—or create irksome feelings among those who do.

Name Your Building

One of the easiest and best ways to create publicity for your building is to name it. When your tenants tell friends and acquaintances where they live, they won't say 2100 4th Avenue. They'll say, "At Lemon Tree over on 4th Avenue." "Oh," the friend responds, "I've heard of that place. It's supposed to be a pretty good place to live. How do you like it?"

> **2100 4th Avenue, Hampton Arms, or The Lemon Tree? Names do make a difference.**

"It's great. We pay a pretty stiff rent, but it's well worth it. Certainly beats most of those rat traps we looked at. The owner really works to make sure everything's taken care of."

Turnaround Name Change Do you recall the airline, Value Jet? If so, you may remember the company because of its lax safety standards. They flew one of their planes into the Everglades and killed everyone on board. Because Value Jet no longer operates, you may think that the bad publicity surrounding that accident drove the company out of business. But it didn't. Value Jet now flies under the name Air Tran.

Take a tip from Value Jet. If the building that you're buying suffers from a poor reputation, dump its present name and give it a new one.

What Name Should You Use?   As much as possible, try to link the name of the property to a theme you carry through in your marketing, landscaping, and building design. Use a name that will appeal to your target market. Avoid names that have become shopworn or clichés. Pick up a newspaper from a large city across the country. Read through the names of the new home developments and large apartment complexes. Find a distinctive and appealing name that you can adapt to your operations.

If your property is old, it may carry a moniker such as "Hampton Arms" or "Mayfair Apartments." These names date the property. Unless you're appealing to seniors, get rid of any name that sounds like it came from the 1940s—unless, of course, you can creatively develop a period theme that combines clever nostalgia with hip. (How about Casablanca with a film noir motif.) Okay, I'm getting carried away. But you do need to stand out in the crowded marketplace. Your choice of names and an overall theme for the property can work magic. (See Box 9.1.)

Ask the Post Office to Put You in a More Prestigious Location   No, the post office won't move your building. Sometimes, though, they will give you a new address, as when a small portion of Miami decided they wanted to name themselves Pinecrest, and Gaithersburg, Maryland, was able to change its name to North Potomac in an effort to share in the aura of its prestigious neighbor. Make no mistake, building names and addresses do count. So much so in some areas that buildings on one less prestigious street will connive to secure the address of another more prestigious street.

> Tenants will pay for a higher status address.

The owner of 466 Lexington in Manhattan connected his building to the property at 230 Park Avenue, and thereby became (with the blessing of the post office) 237 Park Avenue. Just by finagling a Park Avenue address, this owner managed a 10 to 20 percent increase in his rent collections. Figure out a way to obtain a higher status address, and tenants will gladly pay you higher rents—even

One of my earliest large properties was a campus complex of 130 units. When I took it over, only 20 units were rented for the next semester! The problem stemmed largely from location. The project was on the outskirts of the campus area, definitely farther from classes than most housing. Because it was across a bridge from campus, it was psychologically separated as well as geographically.

Because the project had a very low occupancy from its inception, it had suffered from poor maintenance and developed a shoddy, second-class image.

I knew I would have to upgrade the physical condition of the property immediately, but my main concern was how to change the total image. I had to make the property desirable as a place for students to live. Because I could not move the building, I had to make it inviting in its present location.

To quickly create a new and exciting image, I started with a new name, "Campus Highlands," and a symbol in the form of "Scotty," a Scottish Highlander, complete with kilt.

This gave quick visual identification to everything I did in the way of promotion and advertising, and one move just built on another.

No doubt the major marketing coup was the introduction of a minibus suitably identified with Scotty and available for the exclusive use of Highland residents. A driver ran tenants back and forth to school all day, and on weekends we made the rounds of campus bars, hangouts, and athletic events. Now I could advertise as the only apartments that were just a few steps away from every place on campus. In nothing flat, the location problem was not only neutralized, it was turned into a plus!

To get inexpensive attention and build our name, I printed up thousands of miniature bumper stickers featuring "Scotty sez . . ." followed by some risqué remark. It was kind of a student-oriented fortune cookie campaign. Everyone was anxious to read everyone else's "Scotty sez" sticker. They quickly appeared on bicycles, raincoats, notebooks, and throughout the college. Since everyone was asking who Scotty was, the entire study body soon knew about Campus Highlands.

Now that I was getting tenants, I added an amenity that fit their idea of fun. "Scotty's Club" was set up for the residents in an unused basement space as a lounge-recreation area. On Sunday evenings the management threw free beer and pizza parties with special events such as W. C. Fields movies. Pretty soon Scotty's Club was the "in" place on campus. After just one semester, the Highlands was the only apartment complex on campus with a waiting list.

Box 9.1   Investor Craig Hall Tells How He Repositioned Campus Highlands.

> Although this was a very special situation, it is a universal example because
> it dramatically illustrates the most basic of all marketing principles: Relate
> to the needs and desires of your market. Don't look for ideas that will
> work in all properties—there are none. Keep an open, searching mind.
> Seek out things you can do to attract and satisfy the best tenants for each
> specific investment. Then do those things necessary to get them and
> keep them.

Box 9.1   *(Continued)*

though nothing else about the property has changed. In some cities,
tenants will pay more for the right zip code or telephone exchange,
especially now with the proliferation of multiple urban area codes.

Signage

Any building of four or more units should be marked with a sign.[1]
Not just any sign, but a sign that conveys the character, quality, and
distinctiveness of the property. Generally, professionally designed
signs of attractive wood at least $4' \times 6'$ in size. Place the sign in a
bed of flowers, plants, or shrubs, and highlight it at night with an
energy-efficient flood lamp. Your sign and lighting will make the
building easier to find by the guests of your tenants and your
prospective tenants. Naturally, too, the attractiveness of the sign
when combined with your landscaping and the exterior of the
building will further publicize the quality of your property.

Curb Appeal: Summing Up

As a buyer-fixer, I love to find good buildings with rundown exteriors, yards, landscaping, and fencing. Taken together, these de-

---

1. Before you commit to any type of signage, verify the requirements and prohibitions of your local
sign ordinances. Nearly all cities regulate sign size, placement, and lighting. My advice here pre-
sumes legality.

teriorated features lock a negative impression into the minds of most investors. These negatives heavily discount the property's curb appeal and its market (and rental) value. Among all of the improvements you can make to a property, creating dazzling curb (and backyard) appeal will pay back your investment many times over. But, as I have emphasized, you must attend to details.

The Well-Dressed Man or Woman   Think of the well-dressed man or woman. Both achieve that spectacular look by paying attention to a dozen or more details. Hair, makeup, jewelry, color, style, fit, freshly-cleaned and pressed—everything works together. Now, place a stain on a blouse or tie and what do you get? A negative impression. That's what people will remember.

> Which will you distinctly recall: the Armani suit or the stain on the Versachi tie?

How to Achieve That Dazzling Curb Appeal   Unless you're creatively gifted, *great* ideas for improving a property may not come to you easily. They certainly don't come easily to me. I rank high among the artistically challenged. So, here's how I overcame this obstacle.

I carry a camera in the glovebox of my car. Often when I see a building or yard that displays eye-catching features, I snap a picture. Over time, I've put together a large collection of photos. When I'm trying to figure out how to best improve a fixer property and give it curb appeal, I pull out some of these photos and compare a model property's feature to feature with the fixer property. This method always brings forth a rush of value-creating ideas. Try it, you'll like it.

I'll also remind you that you don't necessarily have to rely on your own snapshots. Dozens of "House and Home" types of books and magazines fill the shelves of bookstores. I regularly buy these publications. Their articles and photos will definitely juice up your creative thinking and aesthetic sensibilities.

Collect More than Rent

Look closely for ways to generate extra income.

When you review the income statements of apartment buildings, you will frequently come across a line item called "other income." These amounts may include money earned from laundry machines, parking, storage lockers, and various services and amenities.

Laundry

Ideally, your units will include space for washer/dryer hook-ups. But if they don't, look for space somewhere else on the property to put coin-operated (actually now card-operated) washers and dryers. Without on-premises laundry facilities, your building will suffer a serious competitive disadvantage. Most good tenants were raised in homes with washer/dryers. They are not now wanting to start taking their dirty clothes to a laundromat.

Don't worry about machine maintenance problems. Most owners of small income properties don't own the laundry machines. They contract out the business to specialized companies who then split their take with the real estate investor. You can also lease machines with a maintenance agreement. Then all receipts from the equipment belong to you. Price both alternatives to see which one might prove most profitable in the type of building(s) that you buy.

Parking

If parking spots are scarce in the neighborhood where you own properties, consider an extra charge for parking (or perhaps an extra charge for a second car). Do not arbitrarily give one parking space per unit. Some tenants may not have cars. Others may be willing to park on the street. By pricing your scarce parking separately from the units, those tenants who want it most will pay more.

As with all other decisions, how you handle parking will vary with the practices of competitive properties. Nevertheless, think through your opportunities. Assigning a space with each unit is one possibility. But also explore other options that place the highest value on a scarce resource.

> **Calculate the value of your parking facilities.**

If your site is blessed with more parking spaces than are needed by your tenants, rent those extra spaces to tenants in nearby buildings that lack adequate parking. Also, many car owners will gladly pay extra for covered parking. If your property will accommodate this improvement, the payback will generally create a sizeable return on your investment.

Build Storage Lockers

When you own real estate, you want to squeeze some profitable use out of every nook and cranny within the building, and within every square foot of the site. Real estate (building or land) is much too valuable a resource to waste.

One such profitable use is storage lockers. Does the property include an attic, basement, or crawl space where you could carve out room for storage? You can easily rent such lockers for $10 to $20 per month. Generally, you can achieve payback in less than four years. If no existing space within the building can serve this purpose, perhaps the site might accommodate several of those pre-fabricated storage "huts."

(NOTE: Before you convert any extra building space into paid storage, determine whether you might also convert it into livable rentable space. If so, run the numbers to figure which use could generate the highest amount of net income. Surprisingly, paid storage often provides the more profitable use.)

Cable/Satellite

As the owner of a multi-unit building, you may be able to control access (in most states) to the individual apartments by the cable television and high speed Internet companies. In addition, you may be able to control whether a cable or Internet provider may place a satellite dish on your property.[2] This may possibly add to your building's income in three ways.

1. Buy wholesale, sell retail. Wire the total building and pay the provider a wholesale cost; then charge each tenant a monthly rate with a mark-up.
2. Buy wholesale, sell wholesale. Pass along your wholesale cost savings to your tenants to add to your competitive edge. This "good deal" will stick in their minds.
3. Buy wholesale, include the service with the rent. I do not usually advocate any approach to revenue whereby a special service or amenity is offered to everyone, unless the marginal cost of providing the service is very low and few residents would pay for it. In most instances, you gain more by selling to those who will value and appreciate (no extortion) what you're offering. "Free" seldom pays as a market strategy. Nevertheless, if competitive conditions warrant it, consider adding this perk.

Again, the cable/satellite potential illustrates how entrepreneurial property owners persistently question standard operating procedure. They persistently evaluate what is and contemplate what could be.

---

2. Check with a local attorney. Owing to political lobbying by the cable companies, federal regulators are challenging the rights of property owners to exercise control over their own buildings.

Add Other Amenities or Services

As you read in Box 9.1, noted real estate syndicator and turn-around specialist Craig Hall tells of buying an underperforming property that suffered because of its inconvenient location. Then as part of his strategy to create value, he offered tenants a commuter van. Likewise, whenever you take over a property, think through a list of services or amenities that you could provide (preferably at a price) that would increase your revenue *and* strengthen your competitive edge.

In addition to cable/satellite service, consider services such as cleaning, day care, or transportation. In terms of amenities, would your tenants appreciate (and pay for) a swimming pool, tennis courts, racquetball (or squash) courts, a fitness center, or a study room. As Craig Hall advises, "Keep an open and searching mind. Seek out things you can do to attract and satisfy the best tenants for each specific investment." Amen!

CHAPTER 10

Creative Ways to Make More Money

Up to this point, you've discovered how to choose an area with a stable (and preferably) growing local economy, value a property, and fashion your entrepreneurial improvements toward a selected target market of tenants. But your opportunities to make money with small income properties continue further. Through your creativity, you can also incorporate one or more of the following ideas into your efforts to maximize profits:

◆ Tailor your lease agreement.
◆ Offer units with furnishings.
◆ Improve the neighborhood.

Tailor Your Lease Agreements

> **Use your lease to reinforce your market strategy.**

Most owners of small rental properties draft their leases to focus on "iron clad" terms that require the tenant to pay rent, care for the property, and follow all house rules and policies. As a result, these owners never realize that the lease, itself, can become a powerful part of their overall market strategy.

In fact, leases can do far more to advance your market strategy than they can to force a bad tenant to go straight. You primarily deal with bad tenants through careful screening, not by going to court to enforce a lease.

Don't get me wrong. In these litigious times of tenant rights, you must bind your tenants with a well-crafted and legally enforceable written agreement. I'm not encouraging you to do otherwise; however, I do want you to go beyond legal necessity and consider how you can use the language of your lease to attract great tenants.

Competitive Advantage

Before you decide on the specific terms of your lease, closely review the leases of other property owners. Look for ways to differentiate your rental agreement that would encourage tenants (your target market) to choose your property over competing properties. For example, you might gain a competitive advantage by lowering your up-front cash requirements, offering a repair guarantee, shortening your lease term, guaranteeing a lease renewal without an increase in rent, or placing tenant security deposits and last month's rent in the investment of the tenant's choice to accrue interest or appreciation for the tenant's benefit.

> **Your lease can help you differentiate your apartments from those of your competitors.**

Alternatively, perhaps you could develop very "tight" or "restrictive" lease clauses and position your property as rentals that cater to more discriminating and responsible tenants. You could include severe restrictions on noise and other nuisances common to rentals. In that way you could promote your property as "the quiet place to live."

You create competitive advantage not only by adapting the features of your property to the wants of your tenant market but also by custom tailoring the clauses, language, and length of your lease to match tenant needs.

Explain Your Advantages   By adapting leases to better fit the needs of your target market, you can increase your rental revenues, achieve a higher rate of occupancy, and lower your operating expenses. To fully realize these benefits, though, you must make sure that prospective tenants recognize and understand the advantages you're offering. Adopt the strategy of a successful salesman. Rather than show your property perfunctorily, point out and explain (from the tenants' standpoint) the desirable features of both the unit and your lease.

> **Show and tell.**

Understandable, Easy-to-Read Language   As a starting point, consider doing away with those multi-page, fine-print, lease forms that are filled margin to margin with legal jargon. Instead, work with an attorney to construct a much more reader-friendly agreement. Besides, those excessive legalisms can sometimes work to your disadvantage.

Legalisms bite back.   When you take an overly legalistic approach with your tenants, don't be surprised when they respond in kind. The more pages your lease entails and the more arcane its language, the more likely your tenants (or *their* lawyers) will find some word or clause to argue about. (Lawyers pull in far more money from litigating a lease than they do from drafting a lease.)

> **What good's a lease that no one can or will read?**

Originally, fine-print leases were used primarily to intimidate tenants. Today, that purpose is as outdated as feudalism. Today, if pushed, your tenants and their lawyers can become equally creative in their interpretation of lease clauses. Even worse, your tax dollars may actually pay your tenant's attorney via legal aid, government tenant rights, or human rights agencies.

The myth of a "strong" lease.   Supposedly, a "strong," fine-print lease is one where every clause binds the tenants into doing ex-

> **Bad tenants break strong leases every day.**

actly what you want them to do. (Oh, if it were only that easy.) All too often, though, tenants do what they want to do—lease or no lease. Don't believe in the myth of a "strong" or "airtight" lease. In most cases, it's not the strength of the lease that determines whether your tenants conduct themselves in a manner consistent with your wishes. Rather, it's the quality of the tenants themselves.

A strong lease can never substitute for careful tenant selection. When push comes to shove, a strong lease *may* help you mitigate the aggravation and losses caused by troublesome tenants. But, regardless of the language in your lease, it's good tenants alone who will make your days as a property owner both profitable and enjoyable.

Joint responsibilities? Because ostensibly, most leases are drafted for the primary benefit of property owners, they routinely slight tenant rights and owner responsibilities. In contrast, as part of your market strategy to attract quality tenants, your lease might display a more balanced treatment.

Without a doubt, many tenants do view landlords with suspicion and distrust. If you adopt a more just approach, you will display your good faith. It also will reveal you to be a cut above other property owners. Plus, because you do intend to fulfill your responsibilities, a listing of these responsibilities will help educate your tenants. More than a few tenants believe that owners of rental properties do little more than collect rents and get rich. You gain when you disabuse them of this illusion by listing your responsibilities and expenses within the lease.

Joint drafting? People feel more committed to agreements when they help shape them. To put this fact to your advantage, try discussing and drafting the terms of your lease agreement with tenant participation. Naturally, you'll have a good idea of which clauses, conditions, and responsibilities you want to address. But

> **Ask your tenants for their input.**

some give and take will make the tenants feel like contributing partners rather than mere vassals or serfs.

Win-win negotiating. Joint drafting also can provide another benefit. Your proposed tenant may suggest trade-offs whereby you both win. Some years back when I first moved to Florida, for example, I tried to rent a place to live for a period of three to six months. Before buying a home, I wanted time to learn the market and explore options. But because I desired a short-term tenancy as well as the fact I owned a pet (a Yorkshire Terrier), I faced slim and undesirable pickings. As a result, I stayed at a Holiday Inn for 14 weeks.

Yet, had I been able to secure a satisfactory rental house or apartment, I would have been a perfect tenant. I also would have been willing to pay a premium rent and large security deposit. Yet, all of the property owners and managers I talked with simply stated their "no pets" rental requirement. None even hinted at the possibility of negotiating win-win.

Think carefully before you adopt such a rigid policy. Even if you don't jointly draft a lease agreement, at least keep the negotiating door open. Let the prospective tenants know that you are open to win-win flexibility and mutually advantageous changes. When you ask for tenant input, you discover the issues of most concern and value to the tenant. It's in those instances that you can price for maximum profit, yet still offer tenants their preferred value proposition (PVP).

> **You can boost profits with a flexible, open mind.**

What Terms Might You Negotiate?

Theoretically, you could open up the entire lease to negotiation. That's certainly the practice for leases that apply to some large office buildings and shopping centers. But I fear that excessive flexi-

bility would prove unworkable for owners of small rental properties. In my experience, here are the issues where you might voice
flexibility.

◆ Screening criteria   ◆ Pets
◆ Amount of rent   ◆ Wear and tear
◆ Amount of deposit   ◆ Terms of the lease
◆ Improvements for tenants   ◆ Strict rules

In suggesting these possibilities for negotiation, I do want to men-
tion again that all of your negotiations must take place within the
context of applicable fair housing laws. Generally, you can't steer
the terms of your lease toward a person's race, religion, ethnicity,
sex, age, disability, or any other category that's protected by fed-
real, state, or municipal housing laws.

However, so-called fair housing doesn't deny you the right to
mutually tailor a lease with your prospective tenants. As analogy,
mortgage lenders discriminate and negotiate every day of the
week. They do not, though, discriminate on nonpermissible
grounds. Neither should you.

Tenant Screening Many property owners set one minimum
standard for credit and income. Applicants either pass or fail. This
screening policy will generally prove simple and
legally defensible. In contrast, to again draw on
the analogy from mortgage lending, mortgage
applicants don't suffer the same fate. While years
ago borrowers were either accepted or rejected,
today lenders quote different interest rates,
down payments, and closing costs to hopeful
borrowers who differ in terms of credit quality,
affordability ratios, and job history. In addition, contrary to popular
belief, most lenders will negotiate your loan costs.

In other words, if you have earned a FICO (overall credit profile) score of 780, nearly all lenders will charge you less and ap-

> **Don't arbitrarily
> screen out good
> people.**

prove you for a lower down payment than someone else who displays a 620 FICO score. Would this same tactic work for you?

Good people, bad credit. For example, say you're asking $750 a month and you require a $1,000 security deposit. You receive an application from a couple whose credit score of 575 sits below your cutoff number of 625. They explain that their bad credit resulted from a spell of unemployment. They always paid their rent on time. They really like your unit. They're willing to pay $800 a month and give you a $2,000 security deposit.

What do you do? Do you accept or reject them? Of course, many owners would never get this far. Their rigid minimum would rule this couple out. But it's for this very reason that you might want to set a policy of flexibility—as long as you're compensated accordingly.

Amount of Rent   Some owners prefer not to quote a rental rate over the telephone. Instead, they quote a price range. When prospective tenants show up to look at the apartment, the owner says, "Okay, what will you give me for it?" Well, he doesn't use quite those words, but words similar to those do set the stage for discussions about the amount of rent that the prospects would be willing to pay. This approach can prove profitable for at least two reasons:

Find the high bidder.   You might get a high bid from someone who particularly likes your unit because it offers one or more critically important features that the prospect has not found elsewhere. Of course, that's precisely why you gather market research. You are trying to discover and incorporate these features into your market strategy such that you can extract higher rents, yet provide more tenant satisfaction. If you use the "bid procedure," you could end up with a higher rental amount than you would have dared to ask.

Also, more owners should definitely use a bid process when tight markets or their superior properties yield a battalion of applicants. In these situations, owners typically accept "the best qual-

Twenty phone calls? Fifteen applications? Raise your rents.

ified." But rather than pick and choose from among a number of candidates, let each prospect bid. The unit will go to the persons who value it most highly. As noted previously, in hot markets home sellers use the bid process to sell for amounts in substantial excess of their asking price.

Learn market information.   When you price your units according to bid, you also gain valuable market information. Think back to our discussion about those owners who brag, "We never suffer a vacancy. Our apartments always rent the first day they hit the market." In fact, any owner who makes this claim is really admitting, "We don't know how much tenants would pay for our units. But we do know that we're under the market."

Other owners take a little more market savvy approach. A unit comes on the market; they advertise it at $650; and it rents the first

Bids beat "test" marketing.

day. Three weeks later, a similar unit becomes available. The owners advertise it at $675. It rents the first day. One month later, another unit comes on the market. They ask $750. No takers for a full week. They back off to $715 and the unit rents in three days.

Obviously, the trial and error approach works better than continual error without trial. Nevertheless, had these owners run an auction or other type of bid procedure, they would have learned early on that the market had jumped substantially ahead of where they thought it was.

Gain in down markets, too.   Bids also yield market information on the downside. If you show a unit to 12 prospects over a period of three weeks and get no takers, your rent's too high (or you're marketing the wrong product to the wrong people). When markets do soften, the faster you learn that fact, the quicker you can adjust your strategy. Don't merely complain that your vacancies are caused by a glut of new apartment complexes offering two

| | months free rent. Revise your rents (or features) to re-establish your favorable competitive position. |

> **Bids help weather soft markets with minimum loss.**

months free rent. Revise your rents (or features) to re-establish your favorable competitive position.

Security Deposit As noted, you might vary the amount of your security deposit based on the credit score of the applicant. Or instead of a cash deposit, you could accept a lien against the tenant's car or another type of asset. You might, too, waive (or reduce) the deposit if the prospects will get someone with a strong financial profile to co-sign the lease. (Mortgage lenders use both of these techniques to make loans to borrowers who otherwise would not qualify on their own.)

Especially in soft markets, you must try harder to qualify prospects without jeopardizing your own profitability. Think of all of those credit card companies that have figured out ways to qualify the "unqualified." Or just imagine what type of slump the auto industry would face if these companies only sold new cars to people who could truly afford them.

> **Structure your screening standards to accept as well as turn down.**

Want to bring in more income? Avoid rigid standards. Think of alternative ways to satisfy your financial (risk) parameters. Look for ways to accept, not reject.

Improvements for Tenants You're talking with a prospect who is sitting on the fence of indecision. You need to persuade her to sign up for your unit. You ask, "What is it that you don't like about the apartment? What can I do to encourage you to make our building your home? Are you thinking of some changes that would better suit your preferences or needs?"

Again, this conversation will reaffirm that you're an open and flexible type of property owner who wants to keep the building's residents pleased. But also, when you candidly talk with prospective tenants, they will provide you with many good ideas that you can put to strategic advantage throughout your operations.

"Yes, I believe that if you moved the refrigerator over here, that would make the kitchen easier to work in. Then you could put in a pass-through for the dining room. And why don't you have a microwave hung under the cabinet over here?"

"Great ideas. I'll get these things done tomorrow. We're very pleased that you've chosen one of our apartments and we know you're going to love residing here."

Pets   Many tenants will pay a substantial rent premium for the privilege of being able to keep a small pet in their apartment. The problem for property owners, however, is not so much pet damage to their property (which can be covered by a large security deposit). Rather, misbehaved pets (and pet owners) can annoy other tenants.

No one wants to hear a dog yelping all day because it is left alone in the apartment. No one wants to hear a cat fight at 2:00 A.M.

So, your mission, should you choose to accept it, is to figure out a way to capture the extra revenue that pet owners are willing to pay. Yet, do so with an absolute tenant guarantee that their pets will not disrupt the peace, quiet, and enjoyment of the premises for others. If you can negotiate an agreement that satisfies both of these objectives, you will earn the King Solomon award for shrewd wisdom. (I have at times succeeded, but also failed. Thus, I regret that on this point I cannot relay any firm principles to guide you.)

> **Pet policies will bring in more revenue and create more problems.**

Wear and Tear   So-called standard leases often state that tenants are responsible for all damages *except* normal wear and tear. I would never use such a clause. It invites tenant neglect and abuse. Many tenants believe that soiled carpets, cracked plaster, broken screens, and numerous other damages reflect nothing more than "normal wear and tear."

I disagree. If a tenant properly cares for a property, that property will not suffer any noticeable wear and tear during a tenancy of one year or less. For such short-term periods of residence, tenants should leave the property in essentially the same condition in which they accepted it. Eliminating the "wear and tear" clause will save you money and argument.

If prospects don't accept this condition, I ask them what "wear and tear" damage they expect to do to the property throughout the year. Because they won't admit to causing damage, that usually settles the discussion. If they do come back with a response that will create "wear and tear," I try to negotiate for more rent, a higher deposit, or some other tradeoff. In the end, I don't take a hard line, but I do want prospects to understand that my rental rates do not include an allowance for damages—wear and tear or otherwise.

> **Tenants on one-year leases should not create "wear and tear."**

Terms of the Lease   Do not reflexively set the term of your leases at one year. As I related earlier, many good tenants need a place to live for a shorter period of time and will pay a healthy rent premium for that opportunity. You might even be able to coordinate a weak and peak type of timing. Say you get a vacancy in the slow season. If you leased for a year, you would face a vacancy again next year during the slow season.

Instead, offer a six-month lease until the peak season; or perhaps a lease for 18 months. I know an owner of a 12-unit property in Flagstaff, Arizona, who rents his units on nine-month leases for college students (September–May). During the summer tourist season, he accepts 30- to 90-day rentals at steeply inflated prices (yet still priced less than the better motels and hotels charge—and also less than the time shares).

Strict Rules   Property owners frequently misunderstand the prime purpose of rules that govern tenant behavior. These owners think that rules exist primarily to protect their property. Not true. Look at the long and detailed house rules that govern the homeowners of a $1,000,000 Manhattan co-op or a $2.5 million Long-

boat Key condominium. These rules exist to preserve the nature of
the community. The residents clearly want strict rules because
they are the people who create and enforce them.

The same principle holds for small apartment communities.
Make strict rules part of your market strategy. The best tenants are
those who appreciate tight rules such as rules that pertain to pets,
noise, parking, smoking, cleanliness, partying, and
so on. In other words, you don't so much use
your rules to control behavior. Rather by adopt-
ing strict rules, you appeal to people who con-
scientiously behave as good citizens and want
others to behave likewise.

> **Give the tenants a voice in rule-making.**

Overall, structure your rules for the good
of the residents, not as some punitive dictate of
a feudal landlord. Also, seek input from tenants as to what rules
they would like to see implemented, modified, or discontinued. It's
your building, but it's their home. Give them a voice in how you
can enhance their satisfaction and everyday living.

Summing Up   I have just sampled a variety of ways that you can
incorporate screening criteria, the terms of a lease, and various
house rules into your market strategy. Too many owners of small
income properties never realize how these so-called legal or financial issues tie in with marketing an apartment building. But now,
you can see why you should never adopt a leasing procedure
without explicitly weighing both its costs and its benefits. You can
use the terms of your lease as a means to "target market" in the
same way that you can design the features of your property to appeal to a select segment of residents.

Should You Furnish Your Apartments?

Some owners offer their apartments with everything furnished including dinnerware and bedclothes. Others rent their units stark
naked—not even appliances or window coverings. Most owners
operate somewhere in between these two extremes.

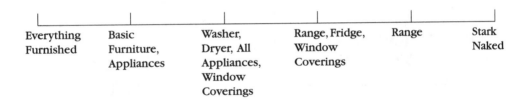

| Everything Furnished | Basic Furniture, Appliances | Washer, Dryer, All Appliances, Window Coverings | Range, Fridge, Window Coverings | Range | Stark Naked |

<table>
<tr><td>**Add appliances and furniture to jump your rent levels and reduce vacancies.**</td><td>Where along this continuum should you operate? By now, you know the answer to that question. It depends on whom you are targeting with your units. It depends on the overall balance (or imbalance) in the supply/demand ratios for these various possibilities. The key to maximum profitability lies in figuring out how much payback you will get as you incrementally add appliances and furnishings.</td></tr>
</table>

All Price Levels

Contrary to what you might believe, furnished apartments (and houses) rent at all price levels (see Box 10.1). Although "furnished" generally implies low end, that's not necessarily the case. In many cities, you will find strong demand for furnished units from mid- to upper-income households. Most of these tenants will own homes elsewhere, or they may have placed their household goods in storage. In either case, their temporarily transient or uncertain situation gives them a need for (usually) a shorter-term, low-hassle living arrangement. Absent a suitable house or apartment, people in this market typically reside in regular motels or extended-stay types of accommodations.

High Payback

Although local markets vary, you will generally earn a high payback for offering some of your units furnished. I have been able to

601
APT – FURNISHED
SAN FRANCISCO

$850 EDWARDEN Studio xtras include sm rm. Gas utils include. Nu renov beaut furn sm antique nr Buena V Pk. Refs 415-431-9987

$900 Fully furn. Studio. mo-to-mo All utils paid. Wkly housekeeping Gym passes.   415-203-2730

$1100-$4000 Studio, Jr. 1, 2 & 3 Bd
PRESTIGIOUS ADDRESS
PACIFIC HEIGHTS HIGH RISE
2000 Broadway @ Laguna
Unbelievable Bay & City Views
Rooftop Heated Swimming Pool
Exercise Facility w/Bay Views
Garage Parking Available
Open 7 days
415-563-6333 or 415-433-3333
www.trinitymanagement.com

$2200 & up Opera Plaza & Daniel B. Ct. Short-term 1 & 2 BR's Prkg. Sec. Pool, gym Pacific Union Co. 415-345-2545

$1375 & Up   Jr, 1, 2 & 3 Brs

ASHLEE
SUITES

- VISA/MASTERCARD
- Fully Furn'd & Accessorized
- Short & Long Term Rentals
- TV/Cable. All Utils. Include.
- One-Site Laundry, FAX

1029 GEARY/VAN NESS   771-7396

$2000-$6500   1, 2, & 3 BR

Best Bay Views, Russian Hill. Doorman, Pkg Avail. Lndry, Maid Srvc. PG&E Include. 1000 Chestnut 415-433-3333 or 415-563-6333

$2200 North Beach 1 Br w/Bay Vu Lndry, Pkg Avail. PG&E Include. Pool 2140 Taylor   885-0333 or 433-3333

$3,500   2BR/2BA DOWNTOWN VIEW, DOORMAN, PRKG
No Fee   **415-775-3090**

$2500/2 WEEKS Nr USF 2 BR 1 BA Vict. Cottage. Garden. Avail. 12/21. Pkg W/D 415-221-1766

Box 10.1   Make More Money with Furnished Apartments.

command premium rents in both upscale and downscale furnished properties. Some of my downscale tenants even rented from me for periods as long as five years.

Because furniture and appliance rental companies now proliferate, you don't see as many apartments offered "furnished" today as was common 20 years ago. Nevertheless, when I recently surveyed local owners of furnished properties, they reported that they faced no difficulty keeping their units rented. When I verified this information through my callback technique (mentioned in Chapter 4) I found that nearly all available units were re-letting within less than a week.

> **On average furnished apartments lease faster, but turn over more quickly.**

Even if you choose not to provide furniture, you may find (as I have) that you can enhance your units with appliances and window coverings. An attractive range, refrigerator, washer/dryer, and mini-blinds might add $50 a month (or more) to your rent collections per unit. When you consider that the cost for all of these new items will run less than $2,000, that extra $600 a year translates into a significant payback. Plus, units so equipped typically rent more quickly than stark naked units.

Warning: Don't Pay a Premium Price for Furnished Apartment Buildings

When you buy an apartment building that includes furniture, appliances, or other personal (as opposed to real) property, value the real estate and personal property separately. Otherwise, you will overpay for the real estate. For purposes of illustration, assume that you're valuing two identical buildings—except that Fairview Manor rents out furnished apartments and Tiffany Hill only offers stark naked units. Fairview yields an annual NOI of $50,000 per year. Tiffany Hill yields an NOI of $40,000. Using our standard cap rate valuation formula, you would value the two properties as follows:

Fairview Manor   *Tiffany Hill*

$$V = \frac{\$50,000 \text{ (NOI)}}{.10 \text{ (R)}}$$

$$V = \frac{\$40,000 \text{ (NOI)}}{.10 \text{ (R)}}$$

$$V = \$500,000$$ $$V = \$400,000$$

What's wrong with this picture? You've just overvalued Fairview Manor because you've attributed $10,000 of annual NOI to the real estate, whereas you should have allocated it to the furniture. You can easily go out and buy furniture and appliances; then simply move these items into the rental units. Value furniture and appliances according to their actual replacement cost less depreciation, such as the amount you would pay if you bought comparable used items from the newspaper classified ads. Value buildings furnished with personal property as follows:

> **Always separate the income from real estate from the furniture.**

NOI (stark naked) = $40,000

R = .10 (or whatever rate applies in your market)

$$\text{Value of real estate} = \frac{\$40,000}{.10}$$

$$V_{re} = \$400,000$$

> **Naïve investors may pay you an unwarranted premium price for a furnished apartment building.**

The value of personal property (as evidenced by the used furniture and appliance market) @ $25,000. Rather than pay $500,000, you should bid $400,000 + $25,000 = $425,000. Never capitalize the incremental income produced by a furnished apartment. To do so means that you will pay far more than the furnishings are worth in the open market. (Of course, when you're the seller, you try to shove all of the income you can into the NOI that you're capitalizing. Some naïve investors do not understand the critical distinction between real and personal property.

Improve the Neighborhood

> **Buy in the most *profitable* neighborhood.**

Nearly all so-called experts advise, "Buy in the best location you can afford; you can change everything about a property except its location." When it comes to apartment buildings, this advice fails for two important reasons.

1. **Income is higher.** Relative to their selling prices, low- to moderate-income properties typically yield higher cash flows than those properties in the "better" areas. For beginning investors, the "less desirable" neighborhoods can provide a very profitable way to start an investment program.
2. **Neighborhoods can improve.** All across the country, once-shunned neighborhoods are experiencing revitalization. Rapidly escalating home prices in what were once middle-class neighborhoods are detouring homebuyers to locations they wouldn't have considered 10 or 20 years ago.

> **Neighborhood improvement pays back higher dividends than property renovations.**

Become a Neighborhood Entrepreneur

If you will help spearhead neighborhood revitalization, you will boost your rents and the value of your property. In addition, you will be able to attract a higher number of rental applicants to your property, giving you a wider selection of tenants.

What can you and other concerned neighborhood property owners and residents do to promote revitalization or, even better, gentrification? Here are several ideas:

- ◆ **Organize a community action organization.** Seldom will individuals show initiative on their own if they think, "What's the use?" By forming a group, each individual acts with the knowledge that others are also joining the effort.

- ◆ **Lobby government.** Insist on trash pick-up, better police protection, more emphasis on criminal prosecution and crime prevention.

- ◆ **Secure redevelopment money.** Cities, states, and federal governments pour billions of dollars every year into capital spending projects for neighborhoods (streets, sidewalks, sanitation, building demolition, parks, playgrounds, trees, landscaping). Put pressure on your elected representatives to direct some of that money to your area.

- ◆ **Upgrade the schools.** Does apathy reign? Do the kids spend more time with sports than homework? Do teachers discipline more than instruct? Do kids learn more on the street corners than they do in the classroom? Then crank up the volume of protest. Work with parents, teachers, administrators, police, and the kids. Push for a voucher program and enforceable performance standards.

- ◆ **Property owners unite.** Form a pact of mutual property improvements. You'll be surprised. After fix-up work begins, it becomes contagious. Personal standards of property upkeep and individual behavior are lifted.

- ◆ **Bring in the code enforcers.** Read through your city's zoning ordinances, building codes, and sanitation laws. When property owners (or their tenants) fail to voluntarily comply, insist that the code enforcers do their duty. As you read through the codes, you will find rules and restrictions that outlaw nearly all types of nuisances from junk cars to old refrigerators sitting on front porches to loud cars, blaring televisions, and unruly domestic quarrels.

The Huge Payback

Neighborhood improvement boosts rents and lowers cap rates.

Most fix-up books written for real estate investors urge owners to create value by improving their properties. As you have read throughout this book, I, too, strongly endorse this idea. But your huge payback occurs when you improve the property *and* the neighborhood.

Say you improve your property and boost your monthly rents by $100 per unit. The market cap rate for similar income properties located in this somewhat down and out neighborhood is 12 percent. After fix-up, your building increases in value by $10,000 per unit.

$$V_{pu.} = \frac{\$1,200}{.12}$$

$$V_{pu.} = \$10,000$$

Now assume that you combine property fix-up with neighborhood revitalization. Your rents go up by $200 per month; but you add still another kicker to the value equation. As neighborhoods increase in desirability (and decline in risk), the market cap rate for the area falls. With renewed popularity, the cap rate now drops to 10 percent (.10). With gentrification, the rents could increase by $300 per month and the cap rate might fall to 8.5 (.085) or lower.

Revitalization

$$V_{pu.} = \frac{12 \times \$200}{.10}$$

$$V_{pu.} = \$24,000$$

Gentrification

$$V_{pu.} = \frac{\$300 \times 12}{.085}$$

$$V_{pu.} = \$42,353$$

Look for "Starbuck's" to help leadyou into neighborhoods poised for gentrification.

To maximize returns, buy in those neighborhoods that are destined to climb up the status ladder. (For more on property and neighborhood revitalization, see my book *Make Money with Fixer-Uppers and Renovations.*)

CONCLUSION

Investing in Action:
The Bayside Apartments

In Figure C.1, you can see the basic description of a 19-unit apartment building that was recently listed for sale near Tampa, Florida. These data briefly lay out for potential investors most of the valuation measures that you've learned throughout this book:

- GRM
- Net operating income
- Cap rate
- Cash-on-cash return

- Per unit
- Price per square foot
- Expenses per unit
- Expenses per square foot

When a sales agent or seller hands you a comparable set of figures, you now will be able to work through the numbers, compare them to other properties that have recently sold, and judge whether that seller has priced his property competitively. If the numbers look reasonable, you can proceed in two ways:

1. You and your advisors perform a due diligence inspection to make sure you know exactly what you're buying.
2. You perform an entrepreneurial analysis of the property.

Due Diligence Again, take notice of the flyer footnote that all sales agents (and most sellers) attach to their property info and brochures:

INVESTMENT SUMMARY[1]

				Current	*Pro Forma*
Price	$600,000				
Down Payment	$120,000	Cap Rate		11.0	9.5
Price per Unit	$ 31,579	GRM		5.1	4.8
Price per Sq. Ft.	$ 77.92	Cash On Cash		14.7	7.3
Net Rentable Sq. Ft.	7,700	Approx. Year Built	1923		

DESCRIPTION

Property: The Bayside Apartments are being sold with the adjacent property, the Bayview Apartments. The Bayside Apartments consist of two buildings of frame construction and were built in 1923. The front building unit mix is 8 two-room efficiencies of +/− 400 square feet and 10 one-bedroom one-bath units of +/− 450 square feet. The back building is a two bedroom cottage of +/− 600 square feet. There is parking for six cars off street; all other parking is on street. **The lot is .23 acres in size and measures approximately 50 feet wide by 200 feet deep.**

Location: The subject property is located at the southern end of Pinellas County, Florida, which is across the bay from Tampa. The city has a population of approximately 245,000 people, making it the fourth-largest city in Florida. The property is in the city at 25th Street and 132nd Avenue and is within blocks of Tampa Bay. **The city, especially the downtown area, is currently undergoing a tremendous amount of growth and revitalization since the Baywalk Center has opened. There are three recently completed condominium projects with prices from $300,000 up to over $1,000,000 that have been well received.**

FINANCING SUMMARY

Proposed New Financing: $480,000
8% Interest: 10 Year Term: 20 Year Amortization
Monthly P&I: $4,014.91

---

[1] This information has been secured from sources we believe to be reliable, but we make no representations or warranties, expressed or implied, as to the accuracy of the information. References to square footage or age are approximate. Buyer must verify the information and bears all risk for any inaccuracies.

(continued)

Figure C.1   19-Unit Bayside Apartments.

(Continued)

OPERATING DATA

UNIT MIX

No. of Units	Bdr/Baths	Sq.Ft./Unit	Current Rent	Pro Forma Rent
10	1 Bdr 1 Bath	400	$475–$565	$525–$590
8	Efficiency	400	$420–$545	$505–$570
1		500	$490	$500

INCOME		Current Rent		Pro Forma
Scheduled Rent Income		$114,936		$123,012
Other Income		$2,580		$2,580
Scheduled Gross Income		$117,516		$125,592
Less: Vacancy/Other Deductions	1.0%	$1,149	5.0%	$6,151
Effective Gross Income		$116,367		$119,441
Less: Operating Expenses	43.4%	$50,544	52.4%	$62,544
Net Operating Income		$65,823		$56,897
Debt Service		$48,179		$48,179
Pretax Cash Flow	14.7%	$17,644	7.3%	$8,718
Principal Reduction	8.5%	$10,146	8.5%	$10,146
Total Return Before Taxes	23.2%	$27,790	15.7%	$18,864

OPERATING EXPENSES				
Taxes		$4,980		$11,730
Insurance		$3,300		$5,7000
Utilities		$16,278		$16,278
Maintenance & Repairs		$10,197		$10,197
Advertising Promotions		$1,441		$1,441
Reserves & Replacements				$2,850
Licensing & Fees		$385		$385
General Maintenance & Labor		$8,945		$8,945
Management		$5,018		$5,018
Total Operating Expenses	43.4%	$50,544	52.4%	$62,544
Expenses per Unit:		$2,660		$3,292
Expenses per Sq. Ft.:		$6.56		$8.12

Figure C.1 *(Continued)*

We believe the information to be reliable, but we make no representations or warranties, expressed or implied, as to the accuracy of the information. . . . buyer must verify the information and bears all risk for any inaccuracies.

> **Verify all sales agent and seller-provided information.**

Although this disclaimer does not relieve the agent or seller of all legal responsibility for accurate and truthful disclosure, it does paint a large gray area. You can never know how a judge (or jury) might rule. You say, "They misled me about their revenues and expenses." They retort, "No we didn't. We told him not to accept our figures. We emphasized the fact that our information might err."

Signed Representations   Some sophisticated buyers try to shift the responsibilities for truthful disclosures back to the sellers through use of seller-signed representations. If the seller says, "The building's in near perfect condition. We've never discovered any problem with termites, mold, asbestos, or lead paint. Our occupancy rate has never fallen below 97 percent. This place practically rents itself. It's a real money maker."

You respond, "Great! I'm really glad to learn that. By the way, you wouldn't mind putting those statements in writing and signing off on them, would you?"

I'm simplifying, of course. In such instances, it's usually the lawyers who go back and forth drafting the specific language of any signed seller representations. And you can bet that 9 times out of 10, the signed statements tone down the promotional puff commonly voiced by many sellers and agents.

Verify, Verify   Nevertheless, even when you do persuade the seller to confirm his representations in writing, you still must verify every fact that's material to your decision. To recap earlier chapters, as a minimum you must check:

- Rent roll and leases
- Physical condition of building
- Square footage of building
- Quality of the site
- Site size, dimensions, boundaries
- Site amenities
- Zoning compliance
- Market sales prices and cap rates
- Market rent ranges
- Quality and intensity of competition
- Target market potential
- The local economic base
- Neighborhood positives and negatives
- Code compliance

After you complete your due diligence, you benchmark the value of the property according to your analysis of its current operating performance. You then persuade the seller to accept *a price no higher than that performance justifies.*

Running the Numbers   For the Bayside Apartments, you can see from Figure C.1 that the seller has priced this property using pro forma rents. The income statement shows that the expenses for property taxes and insurance are scheduled for a big boost next year. To make the net operating income look better than it otherwise would, they're assuming that the investor who buys the property will raise rents by about 7 percent. To their credit, they do admit that the higher rents will result in higher vacancy. As a result, that 7 percent rent increase will only add $3,004 to net operating income.

> Always question closely any pro forma data.

In other words, if you assume no boost in rents *and* a $12,000 increase in expenses, the cap rate at the asking price equals 8.98 percent (.898) or right at 9 percent—which still isn't bad in today's market. Of course, exactly which numbers you use depends on the facts you discover during your due diligence. On the downside, for example, you could find one or more of these negatives:

♦ Market rents are softening. New large apartment complexes are conceding 2 months free rent on 12-month leases.
♦ The reported expenses fall well short of the expenses actually incurred for this type of property. Property shows extensive deferred maintenance.
♦ Unemployment in the local economy has recently risen from 4.0 percent to 6.1 percent.
♦ A nearby company that employs 4,000 people has announced plans to close its facilities and relocate to Mexico.

Or, your fact finding could discover some strong positives:

♦ Market rents are advancing by 10 percent. All major competing buildings are taking waiting lists.
♦ Current management carelessly overspends for operations. You can easily find ways to economize.
♦ Local unemployment has recently fallen from 6.1 percent to 4.0 percent. Fourteen thousand new jobs were created during the past three months.
♦ A new 1.2 million square foot office and retail development just broke ground one-and-a-half miles away from the property.
♦ Virtually no nearby vacant land is suitable for large-scale development of new condominiums or apartments.

The pro forma must conform to your knowledge of the market.

You can only make sense of the numbers after you have put together the facts about the property, the competition, the local economy, and the target market. With those facts in hand, you can come up with the price range current operations justify.

Entrepreneurial Strategy

Your due diligence prevents you from overpaying for a property based on its current condition and performance. Your entrepreneurial analysis tells you whether you can craft a strategy that will make you some serious money.

The Redevelopment Option   Up until now, most of my entrepreneurial suggestions have pointed toward improving a property (or its neighborhood). But also remain alert for the possibility of redevelopment. When the neighborhood moves upscale, the value of the land may overwhelm the value of the building. When that occurs, you want to avoid pumping money into a building that's poised for tear down. Your true profits will come from redevelopment (or selling to a development company).

> **Before you improve, weigh the possibilities of redevelopment.**

How can you tell when an income property is reaching the end of its economic life (even though physically fit)? Value the land separately.

Back to the 19-Unit Bayside Apartments   To envision redevelopment potential, notice in detail how the location of this property is changing. Notice that the area is undergoing "a tremendous amount of growth and revitalization." The sales flyer also reports that (apparently) the area will support multi-unit condo prices "from $300,000 up to over $1,000,000." Compare those facts to the low-end pricing of the current 19-unit building—a mere $31,579 per unit. Plus, this building was constructed in 1923, which may signal both functional and physical obsolescence.

After seeing this picture of neighborhood and property evolution, the entrepreneurial investor begins to look at the land value more closely:

◆ In what price range would this site sell if it were vacant?
◆ What price did the nearby condo developers pay for their sites on a per unit basis?

- ◆ What price did the condo developers pay for their sites on a per square foot basis?
- ◆ How do the condo sites compare to the subject site in terms of size, features, accessibility, views, and the aesthetics of surrounding properties?
- ◆ What type of redevelopment will zoning permit? If not as favorable as it could be, can zoning be changed?
- ◆ If you could build more floors on the site, could you give the units views for which buyers would pay dearly?

> **Always value the land separately from the building.**

If your site analysis looks positive for redevelopment, buy, hold, operate, and spend no more than absolutely necessary for property improvements. When the time is ripe, redevelop or sell and then cash in. In such a situation, the income property itself provides you an ideal way to invest in land without the heavy risks and carrying costs that vacant land entails.

Real Estate Entrepreneurs Outperform All Other Investors

The financial press routinely repeats the mantra, "Stocks outperform all other types of investments." What a joke!

Only Investors Perform

In the first place, "investments" don't perform. No investment offers a return that's independent of the investor. At a minimum, every investor must decide what to buy, when to buy it, and when to sell. Historically, most people have lost money in stocks because they have erred in at least one of these critical investor decision points.

In contrast, nearly all real estate investors have made money because real estate (especially homes and residential income properties) offers a far more dependable and consistent source of wealth. No real estate investor wakes up each morning and flips on his computer to see if his property investments have tanked. As a result, most real estate investors don't buy and sell properties without careful analysis of the properties. For these reasons, over time, real estate investors have dramatically outperformed the folks who trade stocks and call it investing.

Entrepreneurial Real Estate Investors Perform Best of All

> **Sharpen your entrepreneurial vision. You will make money.**

No doubt, passive investors in real estate outperform those investors who choose stocks, bonds, annuities, rare coins, or pork bellies. But entrepreneurial investors outperform everyone. Entrepreneurial investors remain alert to detect emerging opportunities. They combine knowledge, effort, and imagination to create value for themselves and their customers.

As you evaluate properties, ask and answer two questions:

◆ As is, will this property make a good investment?

But far more importantly,

◆ Can I make this property a superior investment?

When you answer an enthusiastic "Yes!" to both of these questions, you will make a lot of money with income properties.

I wish you the best. Should you have any questions or comments about investing in real estate, please telephone me (800-942-9304, ext. 20691) or send me an e-mail (garye @stoprentingnow.com). I enjoy hearing from my readers.

INDEX